A Dog Is for Life

Whenever a man is lonely, God sends him a dog.

Alphonse de Lamartine

A Dog Is for Life

Celebrating the first 100 years of the
NATIONAL CANINE DEFENCE LEAGUE

Peter Ballard

LONDON : NATIONAL CANINE DEFENCE LEAGUE

First published 1990

Published in the United Kingdom
by the National Canine Defence League,
1 Pratt Mews, Camden Town, London, NW1 0AD
Registered Charity No. 227523

Design by Peter Ballard

British Library Cataloguing-in-Publication Data:

Ballard, Peter
A dog is for life –
1. Great Britain. Livestock. Dogs. Organisations. National Canine Defence League, history
I. Title II. National Canine Defence League, history
636. 7006041
ISBN 0 9515892 0 2

Typeset in 11/13 Ehrhardt by Paragon Photoset, Aylesbury
Printed and bound in Great Britain at the Bath Press, Bath, Avon

Contents

Preface	vi
Introduction	vii
1. 'Rouse the country!'	1
2. The soldiers' friend	27
3. New clinics, fresh crises	44
4. 'Heroic and unflinching'	67
5. Out of the abyss	84
6. No respite	117
Index	119

Preface

The text of *A Dog Is for Life* is based on the records of the National Canine Defence League from 1897 to the present day (although there is little recorded information for the years 1891–7 and, with the exception of two isolated publications, 1951–64).

A Dog Is for Life is not a definitive history of the League and nor was it intended to be; it is a brief celebratory account of our first 100 years of work. Nevertheless, it represents the first attempt we have ever made to pull together the many strands of our story into something resembling a coherent narrative.

We are delighted to acknowledge help from a number of sources. Both *The British People 1902–68*, by Peter Mauger and Leslie Smith, and *Reckoning With the Beast: Animals, Pain and Humanity in the Victorian Mind*, by James C. Turner, have provided valuable source material. We are grateful to the RSPCA for permission to use material from *Valiant Crusade: the History of the RSPCA* (and to their librarian, Olive Martyn, for her interest and advice); to the Peters, Fraser and Dunlop Group Ltd for permission to quote from Edmund Blunden's *Undertones of War* (p. 39); and to the family of Lt.-Col. E. H. Richardson for permission to use pictures (on pp. 32, 33, 35, 70) and to quote from *Forty Years With Dogs* (p. 48). The Mary Evans Picture Library kindly lent several pictures.

We would also like to express our thanks to those members and supporters who contributed information and photographs; to Peter Ballard, who wrote the text and designed the book; to Monica Stanshall, whose assistance on the initial research was invaluable; and to Lt.-Col. 'Rosy' RoosmaleCocq, our former Secretary and Chairman, for his helpful advice and above all for his tireless work on behalf of the League since the 1960s, when our situation was so grave. It is no exaggeration to say that, without 'Rosy', this centenary volume would never have been needed, let alone written.

NATIONAL CANINE DEFENCE LEAGUE, *July 1990*

Introduction

It is a great pleasure to be introducing a book to celebrate the centenary of the National Canine Defence League. One hundred years of caring for unwanted and abandoned dogs is really something to be proud of and the NCDL is heading into the 1990s in better shape and with the capacity to care for more dogs than ever before.

It is, however, a sad reflection on our times that our kennels are almost always full, despite our constant efforts to encourage responsible pet ownership, in particular through our neutering campaign and of course our well-known 'A Dog Is for Life . . . not just for Christmas' slogan.

During my twenty-one years as President of the NCDL, many thousands of dogs have been rehomed from our kennels to become loving and devoted pets. One can only hope that the thousands of people who have received such an enormous amount of pleasure from their dogs will help us to educate the thoughtless and irresponsible minority whose actions continue to cause so much suffering and unhappiness.

So, while on the one hand we look forward to another 100 years of tireless work by our members and supporters, on the other we hope that by 2091 our existence will no longer be necessary. I fear this will not be the case, but in the meantime, with your help, we will continue to strive to improve the lot of our canine friends.

Her Grace Lavinia Duchess of Norfolk, KG, CBE
President

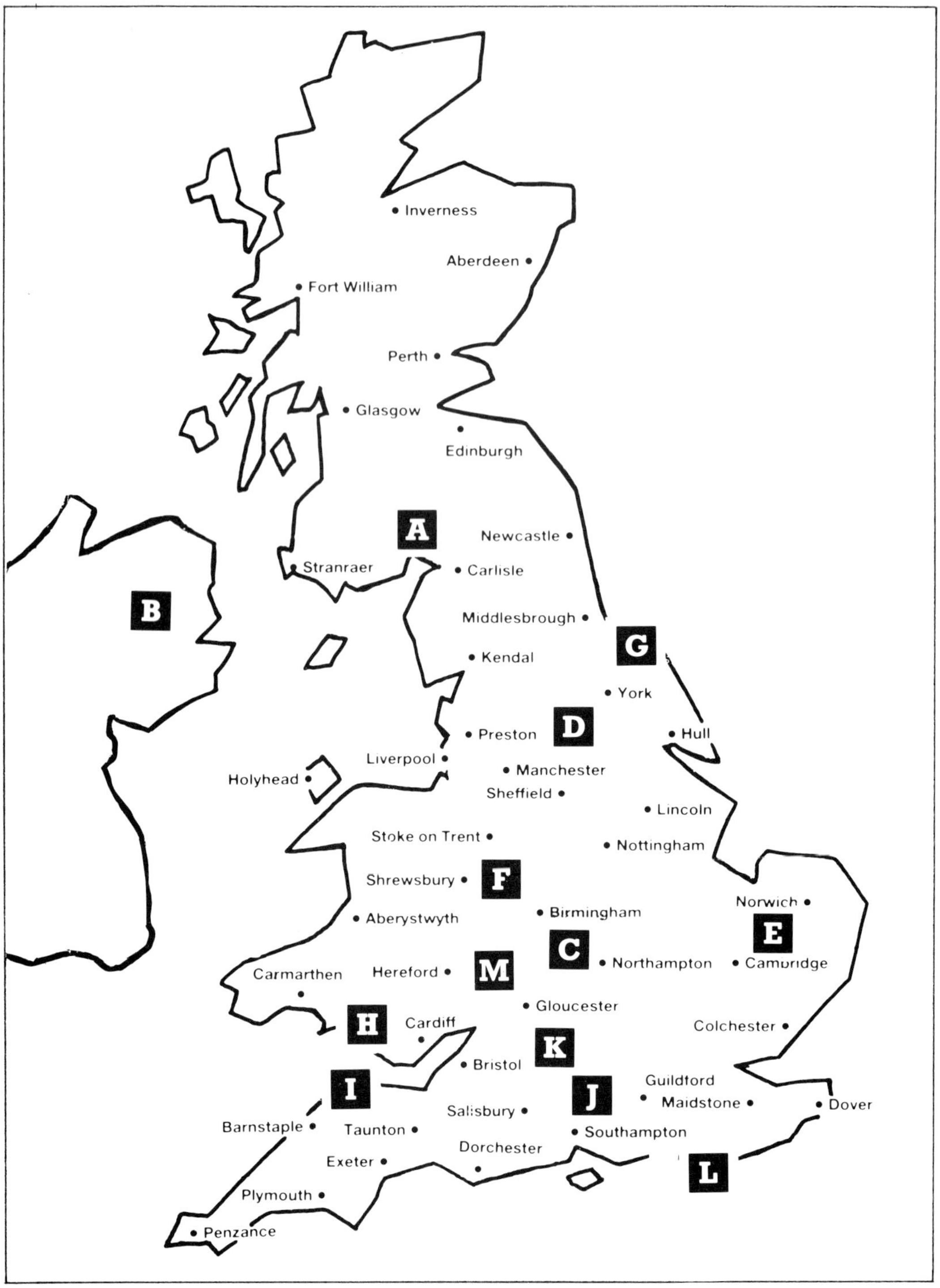

THE LEAGUE TODAY

The National Canine Defence League, as the centrepiece of their vast range of activities on behalf of dogs, runs a network of kennels throughout the UK. *Key:* A) Dumfries; B) Ballymena; C) Kenilworth; D) Leeds; E) Attleborough; F) Telford (Roden); G) Whitby; H) Bridgend; I) Ilfracombe; J) Alton (Farringdon); K) Newbury; L) Shoreham; M) Evesham.

1 'Rouse the country!'

The early years, 1891–1913

In 1898 W. H. Long, the Minister of Agriculture, introduced his first Dogs Regulation Bill, an attempt – and on the face of it not an unreasonable one – to deal with outbreaks of rabies in various parts of the British Isles by obliging all dog-owners to muzzle their animals in public. The Bill would also empower the police to destroy on sight any stray dog suspected of being a carrier.

There had been numerous 'dog-scares' over recent years and Mr Long's department had been active in dealing with the problem long before he brought his Bill before the House. Many people, in Parliament and out, were strongly in favour of the measure.

There were those, however, who saw in it something sinister and unjust – sinister because they regarded the Minister as a longtime enemy of dogs *per se*, unjust because the restrictions which the legislation proposed to enforce would seriously inconvenience owners and cruelly punish dogs without being either necessary or effective. Muzzling, claimed Mr Long's opponents – few in number but vociferous and persistent – was so unhygienic that it was more likely to spread than to curtail the disease and in any case many owners, sensitive to their dogs' comfort, would, as they had done under previous muzzling orders, send them out in muzzles so loose that they would be able to bite anyone to whom they took a fancy.

Victims of dog-bites were offered immediate assistance by the League.

A BUISSON BATH

For the Prevention and Cure of HYDROPHOBIA

HAS NOW BEEN ESTABLISHED AT THE

THE ANTI-VIVISECTION HOSPITAL, BATTERSEA,

WHERE TREATMENT WILL BE GIVEN

FREE OF ALL CHARGE

To Dog-Bitten Persons.

To needy patients, Travelling expenses and cost of Board and Lodgings will be defrayed from a Fund specially reserved for that purpose.

The Buisson treatment is founded upon the simple common sense principle that if poison is injected into a person's veins the best thing to do is to get it out as quickly as possible.

For further particulars apply to

F. E. PIRKIS, Esq., R.N., Nutfield, Surrey.

Telegraphic Address: "Pirkis, Nutfield."

Vociferous? Persistent? No one who roused the wrath of the National Canine Defence League, as the unfortunate Mr Long had previously discovered, could ever accuse them of not making their feelings felt or of wavering in their determination to see a campaign through once begun.

'When the year opened the Executive of the League perhaps scarcely realised to the full the seriousness of the warfare that would have to be waged against official obstinacy and inhumanity,' Secretary Benjamin Bryan had told members in his annual report for 1897,

A contemporary cartoon about the rabies scares. *(Mary Evans Picture Library)*

THE MUZZLING REGULATIONS.
ANOTHER CULPRIT.

the year before Mr Long's Bill was introduced. The Government's 'muzzle and slaughter' programme (as the League called it) was already well under way, culminating in the destruction of 171 perfectly healthy dogs at the Brighton Dogs' Home. Yet the 'dog-scares' which had provoked it were without foundation in almost every case – indeed, in that particular year in literally every case, according to the League, who had investigated all of them with the help of leading veterinary surgeons. (Obtaining the best medical advice typified the League's thoroughness – and its awareness of the importance of a good public image. No one, they knew, would listen to 'cranks'. Cranks who did their homework, however, were a different kettle of fish.)

To combat what they saw as the insidious influence on public opinion of the Government's actions against dogs, the League sent out half a million leaflets and posters putting the dogs' side of the case – which was basically that the familiar expression, 'It's a dog's life', perfectly conveyed what it was like to be one of man's four-legged friends in this climate of hostility and repression.

Mr Long, however, was unmoved and a few months later he brought in his infamous Bill, rousing the League to a new level of fervour. By the summer of 1899 they were able to deliver a petition (or 'memorial', as it was then called) to Lord Salisbury, the Prime Minister, signed by 100,000 members of the public and the medical profession. They also circulated thousands more leaflets and posters; held public protest meetings; employed sandwichmen 'in imposing numbers' to parade outside the Houses of Parliament;

He is very imprudent a dog is; he never makes it his business to enquire whether you are in the right or the wrong, never asks whether you are rich or poor, silly or wise, sinner or saint. You are his pal. That is enough for him . . .

Jerome K. Jerome

and nailed up muzzles alongside copies of the Bill on walls throughout the capital.

The press were mostly on their side and support burgeoned. 'I will oppose the Bill in the House,' one Conservative sympathiser told them, 'you must support me outside it. Rouse the country or we shall be beaten!' It seems incredible that an organisation with a membership of barely one hundred could have answered such a call, but answer it the National Canine Defence League did. A measure described by one newspaper as 'one of the most iniquitous ever laid before Parliament' was withdrawn and W. H. Long later lost his ministerial job (though not his anti-dog passions).

It was the first of many triumphs for this extraordinarily well-organised band of dog-lovers and proved to the world what Mr Long and others had known for some time – that, although they had been in existence for less than ten years, the National Canine Defence League were already a major force in the defence of dogs against prejudice, cruelty and neglect.

'This Society was founded in 1891 to protect dogs from torture and ill-usage of every kind.'

Thus were the League's fundamental aims made succinctly clear on the front of each of their early annual reports. It is a fair summary, but what it does not convey is the enormous burden of work to which this simple purpose committed the tiny band of enthusiasts who started the League. Perhaps the founders themselves did not realise just how widespread was the need for their help or into how many areas of canine life they would have to delve to protect dogs from maltreatment; yet, as you read those reports, you can hardly help being moved by the passion, the vigour, the singlemindedness with which they set about their task.

It was on 12 February 1891, in a room off the Agricultural Hall, Islington, north London, during the first Cruft's Dog Show, that Lady (Gertrude) Stock brought together 'a small party of gentlemen' to discuss the then current spate of 'dog-scares'.

Richard ('Humanity Dick') Martin, the driving force behind the founding of the animal protection movement in Britain.

There had been an animal protection movement in Britain since the 1820s, when the Reverend Arthur Broome founded what later became the RSPCA; but, considering their numbers and popularity, dogs had not done all that well out of it so far. Although the RSPCA was the first organisation to get some degree of animal protection on to the statute books, with the notable assistance of Richard Martin MP ('Humanity Dick'), Martin's Bill, made law in 1822, dealt only with cattle; dogs and other domestic animals received no protection, and this remained the position – with the exception of the easily-circumvented anti-cruelty Act of 1876 – until the League and others achieved some successes in the early part of this century.

It was probably the failure of the Royal Commission on Vivisection in 1875 to exempt dogs from experimentation that finally drove the most outraged of the country's dog-lovers to form their own society. Clearly they felt that dogs, by virtue of what their champions saw as their special relationship to man, were entitled to more protection, and more concentrated support in order to get it, than the existing welfare groups, concerned as they were with the whole animal kingdom, could possibly hope to obtain.

So it was that Lady Stock and her 'small party of gentlemen' came to meet on that winter's day 100 years ago. They were as one in believing that the 'dog-scares' were nothing more than mischief put out by 'persons interested in the establishment and maintenance of Pasteur Institutes' – laboratories in France and Britain dedicated to pursuing research into the anti-rabies vaccine discovered by Louis Pasteur in 1885, for which purpose they sought a steady supply of dogs on which to experiment; it was said that they paid well for carcasses and asked no questions about their source.

The 'dog-scares' led to the persecution and widespread destruction of dogs of every kind, claimed the League, who devoted themselves to protecting not only cared-for dogs but strays, 'who, if they showed any symptoms of illness in the streets, were promptly bludgeoned by the police and pronounced to be rabid'. These were the days before legalised identity discs and collars: many a 'stray' was in fact a much-loved dog who had become accidentally detached from its owner.

The League's earliest campaigns, planned from their tiny offices in London's Strand, were on issues with which readers of this brief history will become increasingly familiar (since for every triumph there were to be many frustrations): the cruelty of muzzling and of prolonged chaining; quarantine and its often sad consequences; the protection of strays; the provision of proper veterinary care; and the iniquities of vivisection and all forms of experimentation on dogs.

Exploiting a new fashion in communication: a League postcard, 1907. *(Mary Evans Picture Library)*

They had good connections in Parliament, with several MPs on their Council, and were thus able to encourage positive legislation and discourage any that seemed unjust to dogs (as in the case of Mr Long's Bill), and they sent out publicity 'to meet every phase of the Dog Question', writing to the newspapers 'whenever an opportunity arose', an instruction successive Secretaries were encouraged to interpret liberally. Among others, the new popular dailies, such as the *Mirror* and the *Mail*, were only too happy to take up a cause on behalf of their dog-loving readers.

Vigour, zeal, dedication, passion, singlemindedness: we are hardly into the story of the National Canine Defence League and already these words have come naturally to mind to describe the way they went about their work. But all this would have been irrelevant without money. Money for rent and salaries, money for printing and

Early-19th-century print of a show at the Islington Agricultural Hall. No one seems to be having much fun!

postage and money for the myriad plans the League had in mind, from paying poor people's dog licences to setting up homes for strays.

Money, alas, was the one thing the League – which has always relied entirely on voluntary contributions – did not have in abundance. Members and supporters gave all they could, but it was never enough, particularly as the League made it a policy never to turn down a reasonable request for help.

The League's pioneers were either too modest or too busy to keep records during those early years, but we know that in 1898 membership was just 127 and income £446, of which all but £56 11s. 9d. was accounted for by expenses. 'A Lover of Dogs' (never identified) had given them £125 in 1897 and others anything from two shillings to five pounds.

By 1899 membership and income had doubled, but so had expenses, notably on the anti-Dogs Bill campaigns. In 1900, appeals to the public for money were less successful than they might have been had various Boer War funds not started up at the same time. Fortunately, 'A Dog Lover' gave a further £500 and so did Miss L. Vernon-Wentworth, one of the League's most consistent benefactors (she gave them £2,000 between 1897 and 1903). The League were able to pay back President/Treasurer Fred Pirkis the £461 he had advanced them from his personal account and still have £14 5s. 2d. left with which to face the new century.

What the League would have done without supporters like 'A Dog Lover' and officers like Fred Pirkis can only be imagined. Fred Pirkis was to keep the League going out of his own pocket for many years, eventually making over his entire bank account in their name.

How to help the League: an early poster.

THE FORMATION OF CENTRES.

Friends can greatly assist the work of the League by the formation of Centres in the districts in which they reside. All that is needed in the first instance is to secure a reliable Lady or Gentleman as **HON. SECRETARY**, and then to communicate with the Parent Society, when literature, &c., will be supplied.

DRAWING ROOM and **PUBLIC MEETINGS** to form Centres can also be arranged if local friends offer or secure use of meeting place and assist in making the meetings successful.

Collecting Cards may be had on application to the Secretary.

In 1902 membership topped 1,000 for the first time, but outgoings badly exceeded income. W. H. Long had not abandoned his hopes of introducing a Dogs' Bill after his defeat three years before and the League were forced to maintain their campaigns against his various proposals while at the same time trying to develop their other work – and also finding, as they would throughout their history, that unexpected crises arose to place an even greater strain on their resources. Outgoings for 1902, for instance, included not only 'Advertisements and Sandwichmen, £313' but 'Quarantine expenses of Soldiers' Dogs from South Africa, £36'. The total debt for 1902 was over £800 and this was to be the pattern for almost a decade as the League was called upon to take arms against an ever-widening sea of troubles.

By 1910 although membership had increased to 6,500, debts had reached an intolerable level. This was the year in which the irreplaceable Fred Pirkis died, by now owed £2,400. His family waived most of this and did not press for the balance, but the League resolved to repay it as soon as possible when they met a few months later for a crisis meeting over finances. 'It has been decided', members were told, 'that in future the League must live within its means.'

And so they did. Within three years they had paid off all debts to the Pirkis estate and built up assets of nearly £2,000, a turnround achieved through continuing increases in membership but also through stringent economies on everything except the service they provided. The Secretary in 1912, for example, C. Rowland Johns, was paid little more than George Knight had received ten years before: £100 – 'hardly a fitting remuneration', as someone had written of Mr Knight but could as easily have written of Mr Johns, 'to a man who . . . has worked early and late, in season and out of season, with his brain and with his heart, as well as with his hands, in defence of dumb animals'. (Despite his frugal start, C. Rowland Johns was to remain the League's Secretary until his son took over thirty-four years later.)

The League soon learned the art of fundraising, organising such schemes as the Million Sixpence Fund, begun in 1904 and designed, they confessed with their usual candour, '1. To clear the Society of debt', but also '2. To carry forward the Parliamentary work for the deliverance of dogs from their torture in laboratories; and 3. To promote the rescue of stray dogs and to establish dog refuges and lethal chambers [for the painless destruction of dogs beyond help] in various parts of the country.'

A Grand Bazaar in Caxton Hall, London, in 1907 – 'patronised by 56 ladies, the majority of them being of high rank' – raised almost £500, while around the country groups affiliated to the League or in sympathy with their aims raised various other sums. Dogs, too, did their bit: with leather collection boxes on their backs, they became a

One of the League's earliest attempts at major fundraising.

NATIONAL CANINE DEFENCE LEAGUE.

Million Sixpence Fund.

SPECIAL APPEAL TO ALL ANTI-VIVISECTIONISTS AND DOG LOVERS.

Two or three years ago, in view of the extraordinary demands on the resources of the League, consequent on the wide spread development of its activities, the Committee were forced to consider two alternative courses of action in reference to the future, and to decide either—

1. To restrict their operations to a few directions, or
2. To appeal to their many friends and sympathisers for their aid to raise **ONE MILLION SIXPENCES.**

They decided on the latter course, and whilst gratefully acknowledging the kindness of many friends who devoted much time and put forth much energy to assist them to obtain this sum, the Committee are nevertheless sorry to state that the appeal did not elicit the response they expected. They therefore venture to renew their appeal this year. **ALTHOUGH THE MEMBERSHIP OF THE LEAGUE IS EVER INCREASING, THE WORK INCREASES EVEN IN LARGER RATIO.**

The League's float in the Liverpool Horse Parade, 1913.

familiar sight in city and town centres.

Only through such efforts did the League survive, but by the beginning of the First World War they were at last solvent and ready to meet any challenge that might be thrown their way. Which was just as well . . .

The League called itself 'National' from the start, but it was six years before it expanded beyond its London base with the opening of a branch in Brighton, where 700 residents had signed a petition against muzzling. Others quickly followed and within a few years branches had opened all round the country, with affiliated groups in Ireland. In 1905 the first of the League's centres outside London opened in Manchester, and soon there were 116 of them in various parts of Britain.

Typical of the work done at the centres (there might be several centres in an area administered by one branch) was that at Liverpool, summarised in the annual report for 1912:

> The 'Dog Licence Club' initiated last year has proved a great success and membership has increased by leaps and bounds [*sic*]. . . . Licences have been given in a few deserving cases. . . . A lethal chamber has been given to the Wallasey police for the destruction of stray dogs. . . . Previously the dogs were poisoned. Good homes have been found for eleven stray dogs [and] eight restored to owners. A temporary home for dogs taken off the streets has been found, where the animals can be safely left as 'paying guests' until provision can be made for them. The Salvation Army . . . cooperated in the distribution of 'Turned-adrift Dog' leaflets in December and January. . . . The Liverpool dog market has been inspected on many occasions and a letter suggesting improvements sent to the market

committee. . . . A board has been erected on a road much frequented by cyclists with this motto: 'Cyclists, remember, you ride, I run. (Signed) The Dog' . . . Representations were made to a large firm reported to have nine chained dogs on the premises . . .

It was this kind of pioneering work which eventually led to the clinics and dogs' homes for which the League became famous. For the time being, the centres – run by members from their own homes – became the 'surgeries' to which local owners brought every conceivable problem for the volunteers to deal with. Those same volunteers also gave full support to the League's national campaigns. Impervious to the elements, to indifference, even to the derision and hostility they sometimes encountered, they went out with collecting boxes, leaflets and posters, unswerving in their determination to do whatever was required to help dogs in need.

And there could be no doubting that the need was widespread. Cruelty to dogs took many forms, from town-dwellers tying them to the backs of trams and cycles just for the hell of it to farmers constantly chaining them up when they weren't working. Dogs were whipped and beaten, sometimes to death, sometimes for no more reason than that they had barked out of turn. They were used for target practice, and in scientific and medical experiments. One was sent down a newly invented tube by the Pneumatic Despatch Company to demonstrate its effectiveness as a conveyor of parcels. The dog was not delivered: he got loose inside the tube and, frozen with terror, had to be dug out.

'*Chained* he is savage and untrustworthy . . . *Free* a playmate and guard': from a League leaflet, *c.* 1910.

A doctor at thc Lister Institute in London wanted to carry out a few experiments into smallpox by injecting dogs with the disease and seeing how, or if, they recovered from it; Fred Pirkis sent a letter of protest to the Home Secretary, and the eager researcher was denied his permit. Another wanted to use dogs in experiments into the causes and effects of drowning. The League pointed out that it was well understood that drowning was caused by an excessive intake of water and its single most devastating effect was that it killed you, slowly and painfully. Did he really intend to inflict such an ordeal on a living dog? Once again, the permit was denied.

In 1909 a sympathetic MP drew the Home Secretary's attention to an experiment at the *conversazione* of the Royal Society in which a bulldog had a spiked collar (spikes inwards) tied to its neck and its feet immersed in jars of salt solution wired up to galvanometers, all in the cause of some experiment or other. The Home Secretary found the whole thing rather amusing 'and richly merited the rebuke administered to him by Mr Swift MacNeill,' reported C. Rowland Johns.

A dog-carriage, from a drawing by Cruickshank.

Owners, too, seemed to find new ways to persecute their dogs, not least by throwing them out on the streets or country lanes to fend for themselves when the dog licence became due (which was in the middle of winter). Prolonged chaining was also popular, as was disposing of unwanted dogs by means mostly most foul.

The trouble about chaining was that to the public at large it didn't seem cruel at all; rather it was a necessity – you couldn't leave dogs to run loose, after all. Quite right, said the League. What you do is train them to obey orders (by kindness as well as firmness), provide them with adequate shelter and food and ensure that they cannot easily escape from the garden or yard even if they are inclined to do so. But it was to be many years before their protests were translated into legislation and many more again before that legislation was given teeth by a test case (*see* p. 40) whose outcome gave magistrates the courage to apply at least the spirit of the law, and sometimes even the letter.

'It is as cruel to chain up a dog as to chain up a child,' said a speaker at the annual meeting of the League in 1912, a year in which over a thousand letters from the League appeared in British newspapers on this one subject alone.

The League introduced their Cruelty to Animals (Amendment) Bill – better known as the Forfeit Bill – in 1908 but had to wait three-and-a-half years to see it accepted, and then only through an unexpected turn of events. The aim of the Bill was to prevent anyone who had been convicted of cruelty to a dog from owning one again. There was already a Cruelty to Animals Act 1876, but, as with so many such laws, there were precious few convictions under it. The Forfeit Bill would give magistrates powers they might be less unwilling to exercise, since the culprit need not – if the magistrate was inclined to leniency, as they usually were – be punished other than by having his dog confiscated, which he presumably wouldn't mind too much, since he clearly didn't find its company particularly agreeable.

As the League told disgruntled members who thought that their friends in Parliament weren't doing enough to get legislation against cruelty through more quickly, 'the amount of time at the disposal of private members for the passage of their Bills is extremely limited, five hours at most' during a Parliament that met only from February to July each year. Every Bill had to pass through at least four stages in the House of Commons, never mind the Lords. 'The second reading debate alone usually takes five hours, and the committee and report stages frequently take much longer.'

Three hundred private members' Bills jostled for attention each year. Balloting among members for precedence hardly helped, with up to 500 MPs drawing for a dozen places. And the 11 o'clock rule, whereby, if there was any time after Government business had been concluded and before 11 p.m., private members' Bills might be discussed, was almost useless: it was rare for Government business to finish early anyway, but when it did the time left before the witching hour of 11 o'clock was usually absurdly short. As Big Ben struck the hour, so the debate was adjourned, often for ever. Trying to get private members' Bills on to the statute book was (as it still is) a frustrating business.

In the case of the anti-vivisection Dogs (Protection) Bill, for instance, which the League first introduced through the MP Sir Frederick Banbury in 1905, in one year alone – 1909 – it was down on the Order Book 120 times, which meant that Sir Frederick (who was to battle on its behalf for over twenty years) had to be in the

A committee meeting, House of Commons, *c.* 1900, from a photograph by Sir Benjamin Stone. Getting Bills even heard, let alone passed, was a major achievement. *(Mary Evans Picture Library)*

From a League poster. 'Spare me!' was the caption.

House at 11 o'clock on each of those occasions in the hope of getting it through to the next stage.

In April that year the Dogs (Exemption) Bill, designed to save stray dogs at least from the vivisectors' knives, was discussed for all of fifteen minutes under the 11 o'clock rule and easily talked out. Supporters in Parliament had thought it stood some chance of getting through and establishing a bridgehead for the main Bill, which by then had failed to get a second reading for five consecutive years.

Two General Elections in 1910, and the death of Edward VII, reduced to zero the League's chances of getting any Bills through Parliament that year, but then they had a stroke of luck: a Bill for the protection of animals generally was successfully introduced into the House by animal welfare friends of the League, including the RSPCA, and the League were able to get a clause inserted in it which embodied the main principles of the Forfeit Bill.

It was a touch-and-go business, though: C. Rowland Johns, realising the opportunity that the new Bill offered, abandoned a holiday in Wales and 'took a sweltering night-journey to London, then suffering from the famous heat-wave. By breakfast-time I had arranged with Sir George Greenwood MP to have the clause included in the [Act].' The Protection of Animals Act 1911 became law in October of that year and at least part of the League's purpose had been achieved: from now on, anyone convicted of cruelty to a dog could have their right to a licence permanently revoked.

The League understandably called it 'a Great Triumph', but the prize they sought above all others, the end of vivisection of dogs through the adoption of the Dogs (Protection) Bill, still eluded them. Their determination to get it through was if anything strengthened by the setbacks they had suffered.

The League had first proposed an anti-vivisection campaign in 1899. 'Our much-vaunted modern civilisation . . . has a very sordid and shabby side to it,' George Knight told members, 'among the worst features of which is the callousness to animal suffering which goes hand in hand with an insatiable thirst for knowledge supposed to be obtainable only through scientific experiment. . . . In 1899 there were 250 vivisectors and 8,469 animals had been used for experiments . . . Thousands of dogs were subjected to most hideous forms of torture – torture indeed which no decent-minded individual would allow to be inflicted upon a beetle or a worm lying on his garden path. . . . Vivisection is a crime and as such should be prohibited (not regulated) by the law of the land. . . . The Society does not concern itself with the results of vivisection and thinks it beside the mark to discuss them.'

Plans went ahead for press ads, the circulation of 'plain-spoken handbills and leaflets', letters to the press and memorials to Parliament, while members and friends were urged to put maximum pressure on individual MPs. A leading veterinary surgeon, J. Sutcliffe Hurndell, joined the League as their adviser.

By 1903 – the year the League moved to new offices in Regent Street – the problem had, despite all the League's efforts, significantly worsened: 232 dogs had been used for experiments at University College, London, alone during the previous twelve months. But now the League, after a great deal of careful preparation, were ready to bring in something quite new, a major piece of legislation: not merely an amendment to the Act of 1876 but an entirely new Bill which would prohibit the vivisection of dogs, full stop. The 1876 Act had, in the League's view, protected the vivisector, not his victims, by hedging its provisions with numerous exemption clauses.

The idea was not without its critics even within the anti-vivisection movement, which was split into a number of different organisations who did not always work well together. A 'somewhat wild and altogether unworthy attack' by the Anti-Vivisection Society, however, resulted only in 106 new members joining the League from among the ranks of the other societies, including the entire Torquay branch of the AVS itself.

The main objection seemed to be that the League, in pleading the special cause of dogs, were setting back the chances of saving other animals from the vivisectors, to which the best answer was to come from H. Baillie-Weaver, a seasoned animal rights crusader, in a speech to the League's annual meeting in 1910, when he admitted to having had precisely those misgivings himself. 'But my fears were entirely groundless . . . [What] the League is really doing is to use a strong tendency of Englishmen to love the dog to extend public sympathy to all animals.'

Prize dogs at the National Dog Show in Islington in the 19th century. Even such pedigree dogs could end up on the vivisector's table.

To support the Bill, the League organised a nationwide petition, something at which they were by now rather skilled. Signatures and donations came from all over Britain and some from abroad. One anonymous donor sent Fred Pirkis a cheque for £100, another a postal order for 3s. 6d., collected in farthings by the wife of an East End cobbler 'for the deliverance of the dog'. The *Daily News* gave its support through a major series of articles.

By the time the Bill was ready to be introduced into the Commons, on 17 March 1905, the main petition – there was a separate one for members of the medical profession – was long enough to stretch from the Houses of Parliament to Highgate Hill 'and thence back again' (for those who don't know London that well, this is about nine miles), while the doctors' had amassed over 900 signatures, shattering widely held assumptions that the medical profession was solidly behind vivisection. As one doctor said in an addendum to his signature: 'I have been much struck with the

The Royal Commission wasn't short of evidence about experiments on dogs.

Q. 1914. Nerves close to the spinal cord divided in seven female dogs (in one dog the whole lumbar cord was removed), and **8 to 14 days after** the nerve roots were stimulated by electricity.

Q. 739 and 10089 *et seq.* Thirty-four dogs partially drowned and resuscitated, under anæthesia. Permission was given by Home Office for **ten further experiments without anæsthetics,** of which two were performed. Inspector says dogs were chosen **"because they were intelligent, which aids some experiments very much."**

Q. 1232. Openings (permanent or temporary) into the pancreas, gastric region and intestines, obstructing the bile duct, pancreatic duct, cutting out glands, etc. The wounds take about a week to heal and the experiment may last for a year or more.

Q. 471/2. Excision of internal organs, *i.e.,* kidney, spleen, etc. Section of brain or spinal cord, and division of nerves with subsequent stimulation. Tying up of arteries and veins—sometimes followed by severe illness.

Q. 806/16. Sir W. Thornley Stoker, the (late) Inspector for Ireland, said " The amount of **terror** a dog

amount of totally useless experiments on dogs, especially in connection with forensic medicine and toxocology.'

The main petition carried over 700,000 signatures and the doctors' over 1,200 by the time the League presented them both to the King, in July 1905. Signatories to the general petition ranged from Princess Mele Barese, the Marchioness of Ely and various countesses, knights and JPs (some of them vice-presidents of the League) to George Radford of Wandsworth, south London, a poor man but a spirited one: he was so sickened by what he had heard of vivisection that he refused to pay his dog licence. He was duly summoned but, through his counsel (provided free by the League), managed to make his protest heard. His fine of £10 was also met by the League, little enough to pay for the publicity it had gained for the Bill yet small recompense for the trouble his action had brought him.

As the League's campaigns brought the iniquities of vivisection to the attention of an increasingly vocal public, the number of canine victims fell.

Both petitions were presented to the Commons by Ellis Griffiths MP in 1906. The vivisectors were unmoved, however. They pointed to the Government's own Dogs' Act of 1906, which gave protection to strays by forbidding their use in laboratories; obliged the police to hang on to strays for seven days, not five, before disposing of them, giving owners more time to trace lost pets; provided for more humane ways of destroying dogs in police custody where this became necessary; and recommended the introduction of bye-laws by local councils insisting that dogs should wear collars carrying their name and address (not all boroughs took up this idea and where they did the League had to come to the rescue of poorer

We are alone, absolutely alone, on this chance planet, and, amid all the forms of life that surround us, not one, excepting the dog, has made an alliance with us. . . . We have not to gain his confidence or his friendship; he is born our friend; while his eyes are still closed already he believes in us . . .

Count Maurice Maeterlinck

owners who could not afford the expense). It was certainly a positive step forward and one the League had a large part in bringing about, for they had been closely involved in the drafting of the Bill. But it said nothing about vivisection.

The Government itself regularly issued figures of experiments on animals which made chilling reading. In the ten years from 1897 to 1906, experiments rose from an annual 8,000 to over 46,000, of which 43,000 were conducted without anaesthetics. Most of these animals (of whom only a small, but nevertheless significant, number were dogs) were eventually put to sleep, but over a thousand were allowed to live once they had 'recovered' from often serious operations, sometimes involving the removal of major organs.

In 1906 a Royal Commission was set up to look into the whole question of subjecting live animals to experiments. As far as the League were concerned, the Commission was unnecessary – the nation had spoken through the 'Monster Petition' and that should have been enough to persuade the Government to act (uninfluenced, of course, by the fact that vivisection was sanctioned and even paid for in some instances by various government departments).

The Dogs (Protection) Bill was reintroduced in the Commons in February 1907, 'to loud cheers in a crowded House', but again its enemies managed to manoeuvre it out. Thereafter it came up again as often as its supporters, notably the indefatigable Sir Frederick Banbury, could manage it, but made no progress. 'There are yet members of Parliament', reported the Secretary, 'who are zealous enough for the continuance of this blot upon our civilisation to sacrifice themselves to the extent of being present in the House at a late hour of the night for consecutive weeks and months, in order to frustrate the expressed wish of the majority of electors in this country.'

Undaunted, the League went on piling up the signatures on their petitions, another 92,000 of them on the 'Monster Petition' by 1907. Meanwhile, the Royal Commission was gathering evidence. Some anti-vivisectionists had been in favour of boycotting the Commission, but the League felt that it should be given a chance to show that it could be fair. Besides, if no evidence against vivisection was presented, it was unlikely that the Commission would find against it! The League therefore sent the Commission a list of 100 medical men prepared to denounce the practice. The Commission said they would see just two.

As if to cock a snook at the anti-vivisectionists and the Royal Commission alike, the number of experiments on animals went up again in 1907, this time to 73,000, an astonishing rise of fifty-five per cent. The League wrote to the Archbishop of Canterbury, asking him to rouse the clergy, and a third petition, among churchmen and lay Christians, had amassed 15,000 names by the end of the year. Meanwhile, signatories to the 'Monster Petition' had reached 850,000.

By 1910 there was no doubt that fewer dogs were being used in experiments, partly as a result of the 1906 Act, partly the outcome of the League's persistent campaigning. But, as H. Baillie-Weaver made clear in that same speech to the 1910 annual meeting, their importance to the experimenters remained paramount. 'Professor Starling, the most eminent vivisectionist in this country,' Mr Baillie-Weaver told his audience, 'said that if the dog was exempted from use in physiological laboratories irreparable damage would be done to the cause of vivisection.' (Dogs were often preferred for their intelligence, which added a particularly interesting dimension to experiments on them.) Mr Baillie-Weaver's long and rousing speech ended on the slightly incongruous afterthought that 'the sooner you get women's suffrage the sooner you will succeed in emancipating dogs from cruelty. (*Loud and prolonged cheers.*)'

The Report of the Royal Commission was not published until 1912. Although it had a great deal to say in support of the League's case for exempting dogs from vivisection, it decided (apparently by the narrowest of margins, the death of an abolitionist sympathiser proving to be crucial) that the use of dogs should be allowed to continue, although only with strict enforcement of the regulations already existing under the 1876 Act, a ruling which brought a hollow laugh from the anti-vivisectionists, since the ratio of government inspectors to vivisectors was now much worse than it had been thirty-six years before. Then, there had been two inspectors to oversee 300 experiments annually; now there were five to cover over three million in more than 500 different laboratories.

John Galsworthy, who wrote a letter of protest to *The Times*. *(National Portrait Gallery)*

After six years, the Commission had changed almost nothing. The League remained optimistic, nevertheless, that public opinion would eventually swing their way and that in time vivisection would be outlawed. There was a moment in 1913 when it looked as if the Government, moving considerably in the League's direction, might allow the Bill to pass; but Sir Frederick Banbury, still fighting the League's corner with the help of Col. A. R. M. Lockwood and other staunch supporters, in the end decided that the amendments the Government wanted to make to it would emasculate it to an intolerable degree, and he withdrew the Bill to present it the following year.

John Galsworthy was among many public figures who nailed their flag to the anti-vivisection mast, in his case in a letter to *The Times*. But the vivisectionists, too, felt they had right on their side, certain that the advancement of medical science depended on the freedom to use animals, including dogs, in the laboratory. The League harboured no illusions about how difficult it would be to convince them otherwise.

* * *

Dogs, like humans, have rights, the League kept reminding the world, and nowhere more obviously than on the Queen's highway. They made it their business to remind the road-user of his responsibilities to his canine fellow-travellers.

'The League', wrote George Knight's predecessor, John Hughes, in 1899, 'has done what it can to lessen the evil, especially during the recurrence of the Gordon-Bennett motor races.' A member's suggestion that all vehicles should be made to carry cow-catchers at the front was well received. '[It] will be laid before a clever, practical engineer', reported Mr Hughes, 'for expert opinion.' A clever,

The 'scorcher-motorist' was a new enemy against whom the League was quick to act. *(Mary Evans Picture Library)*

practical engineer may well have been found, but if he was he clearly looked in the direction of the growing number of vehicle manufacturers, realised which side his bread was buttered and told the League that, in his expert opinion, such an idea was not feasible. At any rate, nothing more was heard of it. Yet 'not a town, not a village nor even a country road but has its pitiful death-roll of faithful, loving dogs done to death by the wheels of the Scorcher-Motorist,' said the League. When they protested to the Automobile Club,

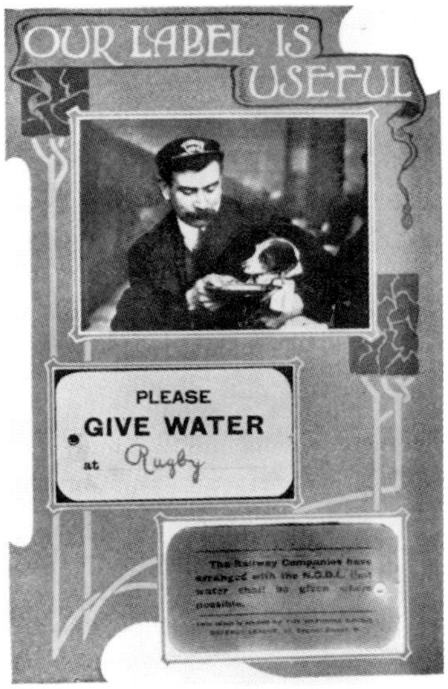

The League persuaded railway companies to provide drinking water for suitably labelled dogs.

their complaint 'elicited some reprehensible letters from sundry automobilists'.

The relationship between dogs and the railway companies went back many more years and had been enshrined in a series of regulations, but the League had to keep a watchful eye to see that dogs' rights were not eroded. In 1900 they reminded the companies that good fares were paid for dogs and they were entitled to 'special sanitary and humane compartments', as well as drinking water, and that 'they should be treated as passengers and not as baggage,' on which subject a petition signed by 20,000 owners was presented by George Knight to the Conference of Railway Superintendents in 1903, seeking the end of the 'dog-locker' in luggage vans and its replacement by simple kennels 'which could be utilised for carrying parcels when not required for dogs'. Passionate but practical: this was the League's invariable approach to any problem, and it usually paid off.

The companies agreed to provide water for dogs 'provided only that a label is attached to the dog, bearing the words "Please give my dog water".' The League designed their own label for the purpose.

In Manchester in 1912 a dog-dealer received two months for packing a dog into a box far too small for it during a long train journey, setting an example which the League welcomed, for such treatment was all too common.

The muzzling orders which W. H. Long had imposed in the early 1890s were finally withdrawn in England in October 1899, but quarantine regulations for imported dogs, imposed at the same time, were not. The League protested to Lord Salisbury. They felt that a vet's certificate confirming that a dog was healthy should be sufficient to get it released much earlier – six weeks or two months was the most that most medical opinion considered necessary. They pointed out the difficulties soldiers returning from South Africa were having bringing their pets back into the country. It wasn't just the length of the quarantine, it was the cost of it – from 5s. to 10s. a week in the Department of Agriculture's Beddington, Croydon, kennels, prohibitive for soldiers from poorer families. The Board pointed out that only dogs acquired very recently in the Cape had to stay at Beddington; others could be privately housed.

This was an unhelpful response: it cost at least as much to board a dog in a private kennel as it did to leave it at Beddington. The period of quarantine itself must be modified, said the League. After all, the Cape was officially rabies-free.

The Board replied that a 'very large number of persons have gone to South Africa during the past twelve months from all parts of the world' (an odd way to refer to the outbreak of war); there were no restrictions on the import of dogs into the Cape, so rabies could

A messenger dog in South Africa during the Boer War (1899–1901).

occur there at any time under these 'disturbed conditions', whatever the 'official' position might be, and be transported to Britain via returning soldiers' dogs, especially as 'in many cases the supervision which owners have been able to exercise over their dogs has been necessarily very slight'.

This letter was sent to Fred Pirkis with an almost palpable air of self-congratulatory handwashing. Such confidence was misplaced. 'Quarantine upon *surmise* is a new departure in Government legislation,' observed Mr Pirkis, and, pausing only to set up a fund to finance the payment of soldiers' quarantine bills, he continued to pursue the Board with all the vigour at his command. 'When veterinary experts expressly assign six weeks as the utmost period that the very rare disease of rabies has been known to lie dormant in a dog's system,' he wrote to the Board, 'the hardship of prolonged quarantine for dogs for six months, or even three [a reduced 'sentence' permitted recently acquired dogs who had not landed at a foreign port during the homeward journey], becomes apparent.' This was another battle which seemed likely to become a case of trench warfare rather than swift victory.

Duplicated messenger service: a messenger dog carrying a pigeon to a pre-arranged point for release.

One of the League's major concerns from the day it was founded was that no one who clearly cared for their dog should be prevented from keeping it just because they were poor. It quickly became clear that a perennial problem was going to be the 7s. 6d. dog tax, which became due every New Year. The Dog Licence Fund, which was to be such a boon to so many poorer owners, was not started until 1910, but long before that the League was willingly paying the tax for anyone whose circumstances warranted help. When they finally decided to start a special fund – general funds being in a particularly parlous state around this time – it turned out to be one of their most memorable contributions to the welfare of dogs in this country, for without it many more pets would have been thrown out in the depths of winter to join the armies of half-starved strays that roamed the streets of all our cities and large towns.

Characteristically, however, the League first reminded owners where their duty lay in law as well as in conscience. In December 1907, just before licences had to be renewed for 1908, they persuaded all 168 Chief Constables in Britain to post notices, 'in type capable of being easily read by passers-by', reminding owners about the terms of the 1906 Dogs' Act, under which it could be an offence not to put an identity collar on a dog so that if it was picked up its owner could be traced and either comforted or ticked off, depending on his reaction.

You may ask why the League were so willing to pay for licences when they hardly had two halfpennies to rub together; if people couldn't afford to look after a dog, surely they should give it up rather than plead for charity? The League, though, saw it differently: people became greatly attached to their dogs and dogs to their owners and it was their collective right not to have such friendships severed merely over a question of money. They recognised that dogs could be as loved in a Liverpool back-to-back, a London slum or a farm labourer's cottage as in a comfortable middle-class home. Provided the dog didn't want for affection, the League was glad to do all it could to help in other areas of need.

A soldier and his dog. Many soldiers received help from the League after the Boer War, especially with quarantine and licences.

An example of almost Dickensian poignancy was that of the small south London boy, almost blind, who just before Christmas 1908 made friends with a stray; the dog followed him home and would not be turned away. Though his parents were poor they took the dog in and he quickly became one of the family. Almost as quickly, however, came a summons for the father and a fine for keeping a dog without a licence. He couldn't pay either fine or tax and the household goods, such as they were, were about to be sold under a distress warrant when the League stepped in and settled both accounts. They could simply have removed the dog and found it 'a good home'. But why, when it clearly had one already, despite the poverty of the surroundings? They paid the tax again the following year.

'Your Committee are resolved', C. Rowland Johns told members when launching the Licence Fund, 'that nothing shall be wanting on their part for the good of the canine race . . . To plead for the voiceless, to protect the defenceless: these are our tasks.'

By 1912 Dog Licence Clubs were starting up in which subscribers saved 7s. and the League paid the 6d. balance, sending the licences out themselves, with the agreement of the local authorities. These sixpences, together with the 137 licences for which the League found all the money that year, came out of the Licence Fund, which was to really come into its own during the First World War.

Even today, in our supposedly enlightened society, the problem of stray dogs remains a serious one. In the early years of this century, when the League first turned its full attention to it, it was unmanageable. In a typical year, 1910, the Battersea Dogs' Home (official title 'The Battersea Home for Lost and Starving Dogs') took in 25,000 strays from the streets of London alone.

The League's first step was to ask members to organise a series of private shelters. It was an easy matter, they said, to find someone who would set up a kennel or two in his garden (the League had small kennels of their own for sale for 10s. and ones large enough for a St Bernard for 25s.) and board dogs for, say, 2s. 6d. or 3s. a week (which members would pay out of their own pockets) until the owner could be traced or a new one found. If the worst came to the worst, the dog could be humanely destroyed under the League's protective eye. In the meantime, the strays would be properly housed and fed and be cared for by qualified vets approved by the League.

Some dogs came into police hands through court cases against cruel owners, something the League had fought for but which, if they themselves didn't get to hear of the case, could leave an innocent dog facing the same fate as genuine strays (and stolen dogs), which as often as not was the auction-room, where they might end up in someone's hands for a few pence, perhaps to be thrown out at licence-time or sold to vivisectors. If the League did get to hear of a case such as the one in 1903 in London in which a thief was convicted of stealing eleven dogs, they would contact the police, circulate leaflets and put ads in the press to try to trace the owners and, if all that failed, try to buy the dogs from the police.

It was always difficult for owners of lost dogs to trace their pets, since they could be in one of any number of police-sanctioned veterinary yards around the city and its suburbs, depending on where each dog was picked up (Battersea Dogs' Home was used officially only for dogs in the county of London). The problem was made worse by the fact that the police only had to wait three or four days before disposing of dogs in their care.

The League printed a list of known yards in London's newspapers once a month, but unless an owner moved fast his pet would be dead or sold before he could get to it. Through the 1906 Dogs' Act, the League managed to get the period of 'grace' increased to seven days, still not enough in a city the size of London. They also offered

Strays outside the League's Manchester centre, *c.* 1910.

A typical dog hero: Baccy with his mistress in 1913. He saved them both by warning her of a fire which had started while she was asleep.

to pay for the publication on a regular basis of lists of lost and found dogs, but the police turned this down on the grounds that the paperwork (for them) would be too time-consuming.

Members of the League in London who lost their dogs were advised to try not only the police and the Battersea home but also such places as Club Row market, Bethnal Green (where every Sunday morning stolen dogs were offered for sale) and local animal dealers – 'it is wiser, however, to call upon these dealers as a *purchaser* . . .'

In December 1912 the League opened their own shelter for strays at Salisbury House, Sherbrooke Road, Fulham, west London, to which they invited, free of charge, unwanted dogs as well as strays and from where they established a system of not only finding a dog a new home but of visiting it afterwards to see that all was well, canine social work of a high order.

Before a dog was allowed to leave the shelter, a guarantee had to be signed by the new owner that the dog would not be chained; would, if ill, receive skilled treatment; would not be used in experiments of any kind; would not be disposed of without the League's consent; would always wear an identity collar (collars and leads were on sale at the shelter); and would be surrendered to the League if any of these conditions were broken. He or she also had to agree to regular League inspections of both dog and its surroundings. The previous owners were charged around 3s. when the League found a new home for their dog through the shelter.

A London street market, *c.* 1900. Dogs were frequently sold in such markets, sometimes for a few pence, with little regard for their future. *(Mary Evans Picture Library)*

LETHAL CHAMBERS.

The attention of the members of the League is called to the urgent necessity for the painless destruction of diseased and incapacitated dogs, by means of a properly constructed Lethal Chamber.

The Committee have paid special attention to this question, and are now in a position to announce that they have made arrangements with Messrs. J. Luker and Co., of Cheltenham, by which such chambers may be supplied at a very small cost as follows:—

	£	s.	d.
(1) Constructed with ordinary wood, and necessary fittings, suitable for any dog up to collie size	5	5	0
(2) Same size as No. 1, superior wood and fittings	9	10	0
(3) Large size, same wood as No. 1, suitable for any size of dog	18	10	0
(4) Same size as No. 3, with superior wood and fittings	25	0	0

Every Local Authority should be strongly urged in the interest of humanity to supply the Police with some such method of humane destruction. From enquiries made by the Committee, it is evident that some of the methods employed by the Police for this purpose are most unsuitable and cruel. The price at which these chambers are supplied are so reasonable, that no Authority should feel that it is incurring any grievous burden on the ratepayers by procuring one.

All further particulars can be obtained on application to Benj. Bryan, Secretary, 27, Regent Street, S.W.

If dogs had to be destroyed, it should be done painlessly, insisted the League, who devised their own purpose-built chamber.

Norah Pirkis, wife of the late Fred Pirkis, had run the League's campaigns on behalf of strays virtually singlehandedly for years; now she was given her own sub-committee. 'This wide extension of the work will mean much additional expense,' wrote C. Rowland Johns, 'but we confidently expect that such valuable service to our dogs will meet with the approval of our members.'

Where it was necessary – as it often was – to destroy a stray whose health was beyond saving or who could not be kept in care any longer, the League worked to ensure that this was done with the minimum of distress to the dog. One method was to administer prussic acid (Scheeles'), which could be bought at the chemist's for a shilling ('insist that the poison should be freshly made'). But, as John Hughes had told members in 1904, 'It is obvious that an organised plan for [the destruction] of unwanted stray dogs is needed for other large cities and towns besides London. The sufferings which these poor animals endure should not be possible in a country which has reached the pitch of civilisation which England has attained.'

The League's answer was a 'lethal chamber', which came in sizes according to need and cost £25; it ensured an instantaneous and painless death.

* * *

It has already been said that cruelty to dogs took many forms, not all of them obvious even to a sympathetic observer. One area in which the League pioneered a change of public attitude was that of the performing dog. People who laughed at and applauded the antics of dogs and other animals on stage or in the circus ring managed not to recognise that many of the tricks these animals were required to perform for their amusement were in themselves cruel and required a great deal of equally cruel training. The League wrote regularly to the newspapers, demanding a total ban on dogs in music-halls and calling on everyone who shared their objections to 'either turn their backs and leave the hall, or not to go to a hall where such performances are billed.' A pledge was signed by hundreds of such objectors and in 1913 a circus at the London Opera House was closed down by their actions. A mass meeting, sponsored by the League, among others, was held at Kensington town hall; a group of animal trainers who turned up to debate the issue 'were badly defeated . . .' Before very long, said Mr Johns, 'dog "turns" on the stage and in circuses will be totally suppressed.'

Whipped, beaten, maimed, trapped, poisoned, kicked out, run over, starved, muzzled, curfewed (or they would have been under one of W. H. Long's proposed dogs' Bills): who would have been a dog in those days? No wonder they sometimes turned on their human masters and took a chunk out of them; the occasional 'dog-scare' was the least their persecutors deserved.

Dr St Vincent-Ryan and Grissel, winner of the League's medal in 1913 for rescuing a 3½-year-old boy from a pond in Wandsworth, London.

Yet while down the road and round the corner a man might be kicking his dog half to death because his wife hadn't got his tea ready, somewhere else someone would be risking his life to save some scrap of a mongrel. The League, forever fighting cruelty, were as quick to recognise kindness and bravery.

In 1901 they gave a guinea each to five people, including a boy of twelve, for rescuing dogs from quarries, rivers, fires and other hazards. By 1904 a framed, illuminated card of thanks went with the cash to such men as Mr Mansell of Begelly, South Wales, who went down a ninety-feet disused mineshaft to rescue a sheepdog; Charles Morgan, bricklayer's labourer, of South Norwood, who 'interfered and stopped the cruel beating of a dog by its master – a gentleman'; and Messrs Palmer and Moor, of Yelverton, Devon, who dug non-stop for four hours to rescue a dog from a disused drain.

In 1906 G. W. Steel, a pit manager, went down on a looped rope into a 540-feet pit shaft three-quarters filled with water to rescue a dog who had been chucked down the shaft by its owner but had managed to crawl from the water on to a narrow ledge, where it had lain in the cold and darkness for two days before being heard. In 1910 James Arnold, a sixteen-year-old from Cowes, Isle of Wight, received a silver watch and an illuminated address for swimming out

Another canine hero, Lassie, with the seaman whom her licking restored to life after his ship had been sunk in 1914.

into the Solent to rescue a terrier being carried away by the tide.

By 1912 the reward was the coveted Silver Medal of the League, and none deserved it more than Edward Raper, mate of a North Shields trawler, who in 1913 swam to the rescue of the ship's dog, with not only rough seas to contend with but a number of voracious-looking sharks. In the North Sea? Never mind that, we can hear Mr Draper saying, a shark's a shark, wherever you come across him.

Now and then men did more than risk their lives. The reward to William Cockerell in 1908 for trying to rescue a dog was given to his widow when man and dog perished together in the cold, deep waters of a Staffordshire quarry.

There were dog heroes, too, notably the extraordinary Don, a retriever from Aberdeen 'and a splendid-looking fellow', who in October 1904 jumped into the sea during a gale to retrieve a rope from a foundering German schooner and carry it to the shore so that the crew could escape. 'Time after time it was thought that he must be swept away, but still he struggled on, reached the ship and, snatching the rope thrown to him by the almost despairing men,

In 1912 these miners from Ruabon, North Wales, rescued a terrier from a disused pit shaft where it had been marooned for eleven days. The lucky dog is shown in the arms of a local League member after a presentation of League medals to his rescuers.

turned and swam back to the shore, where he dropped, in a pitiable state of exhaustion, at his master's feet.' It took Don a long time to recover from his ordeal, but when he did the League gave him an inscribed silver collar and hung his portrait in their offices.

Another silver-collar winner rescued a two-year-old child from a quarry in Lancashire, while Mick, who lived in a Hatfield, Hertfordshire, brewery, aroused his master in the middle of the night 'by rolling his head again and again, in this eccentric manner announcing that the brewery was on fire and thus saving his master's life'. Major, of unspecified breed, typified many dogs by nagging a police constable to follow him and leading him to his master, buried in the debris of a collapsed building in Glasgow.

A dog-hero under fire was Bobs, whose master served in the Boer War and had Bobs alongside him throughout. Bobs 'was able to

Ambulance dogs at a field station during the Boer War. *(Kennel Club)*

render invaluable aid in finding the wounded and giving them succour in the shape of stimulant, bandages and other adjuncts of "First Aid" which could be applied by the wounded soldier'. He could go where the ambulancemen dared not and saved a number of lives through his courage and intelligence. When water was scarce, it was Bobs who, water-bottles strapped to his body, went off and found it. How did he fill the bottles, having not a single pair of hands? 'When he found a pool or stream he would dash into it and revel in luxury, the bottles would fill, and he would return . . . to the parched soldiers.' Bobs was part of a tradition which saw dogs filling many valuable roles in wartime; later generations were to serve with distinction in two world wars.

The original caption to this picture, taken in 1911, put it well: 'A North of England Working-man who has thrice saved the life of the dog which appears by his side. They are inseparable companions.'

With universal education having been introduced in the 1890s, the League were quick to take advantage of the presence in schools of most of the country's next generation of dog-owners, persuading teachers right across the country to distribute leaflets such as their 'Kindness to Dogs' and to inculcate in the children the right, caring attitude towards animals of all kinds. At the 1911 annual meeting, Sir George Kekewich, a League stalwart for many years, suggested that every class should have at least one lesson a week devoted solely to man's duty to animals. There was never much chance of that happening, but this is not to gainsay the worthiness of the idea.

Education was certainly needed: for every adorable picture of 'child with faithful friend' one could just as easily have been taken showing 'dog after meeting unkind child', a firework tied to its tail or thorns driven through its ears.

The careful cultivation of the press helped the teaching process. As children were hearing in schools about the rights and needs of animals, so their parents were reading about the animal welfare movement's continuing campaigns, and in particular seeing stories about the League and their work on behalf of dogs almost as often as they picked up their newspapers. On the whole, the papers were on

Artistic commemoration in the 1914 annual report for two heroes, Harbourmaster T. H. Jackson *(top)*, who saved a dog from drowning at Bridlington, Yorkshire, and John Charge *(below)*, who saved a Hampshire dog from a similar fate.

the League's side, as the headline 'Hearty thanks to the Press' in the annual report for 1900 suggests. 'At various important junctures of the League's political work,' wrote the Secretary of the day, George Knight, 'letters, leading articles and remonstrances have appeared in over 220 papers.'

The League's gratitude to the press never reached the level of unctuousness, however. Although they acknowledged that all the leading national and provincial daily and evening papers had contributed to their cause in one way or another, as had 'various high-class Magazines and Reviews', they had no hesitation in 1908 in rebuking the *Daily Mail* and the *Morning Post* for what the League regarded as their partiality over vivisection. In the *Mail*'s case the rebuke took the embarrassing form of a petition signed by 2,000 of its own readers. The outcome, C. Rowland Johns was able to tell members, was 'a better hearing . . . accorded to the advocates of your League's views'. Even press barons were not immune to the scorching fire of the League's disapproval.

Thus it was – though the story is inadequately told in these few pages – that the League established themselves as the respected champions of the canine world. 'Whatever concerns the dog concerns us,' they said at the outset, going on to prove it beyond argument, despite those twin obstacles they so frequently found themselves up against: a shortage of money and the assembled forces of the anti-dog lobby.

But in August 1914, as the echo of the assassin's bullet died away in Sarajevo, to be replaced by the massed guns of some of the most formidable armies in history slugging it out on the ruined fields of Europe, they found themselves facing a new set of challenges, tests of their resolve and endurance such as even they had never encountered before.

. . . to man he looks, in all his necessities, with a speaking eye for assistance; exerts for him all the little service in his power with cheerfulness and pleasure; for him he bears famine and fatigue with patience and resignation; no injuries can abate his fidelity; no distress induce him to forsake his benefactor . . . in him alone fawning is not flattery. How unkind then to torture this faithful creature, who has left the forest to claim the protection of man! How ungrateful a return to the trusty animal for all his services!

Oliver Goldsmith

2 The soldiers' friend

The First World War and its aftermath, 1914–1921

'The year 1914 has been an eventful one for most people in this country,' begins the annual report for the year of Sarajevo with notable understatement.

It would be easy at this distance in time to mock the League's concentration on the wellbeing of maltreated dogs while across the Channel men were being just as cruelly treated and in far greater numbers. But this would be to misrepresent the importance placed on their activities during the war by thousands of people happy to acknowledge a debt to them, including many men at the front. Far from being superfluous, the work of the League took on a new urgency. Staff was increased, bigger premises had to be found. The workload became enormous. 'There will be very little for your League to do now,' someone said when war was declared. How wrong they were. Old problems persisted, new ones arose. At one point, the very existence of the dog, at least as a family pet, came under official threat.

Dockgateman George Clague *(standing)*, who rescued his dog Scott, also pictured, from the Mersey in 1913.

In all wars, the populace left behind when the soldiers go off to fight strives to preserve what it can of the values, the virtues, the familiar comforts which its husbands, sons and brothers are fighting to defend, so that when they come home the men – the boys – will see that their endurance was not in vain, that the life they left behind is there to welcome them back, to remind them of love, not death. The home fires have indeed been kept burning. Here are the family, the friends, the treasures of peacetime, just as they have been remembered in the trenches.

For many men in the Great War their friends included their dogs: they wrote home asking about them, they worried about them. And for many grieving widows and mothers, the family pet was a vital – sometimes the only – comfort.

The League recognised this, while others did not. At the outbreak of war, amid a frenzied rush to stock up on food, poorer servicemen's families were advised to get rid of their dogs, which would otherwise, it was claimed, consume precious resources. The League's reaction was swift and, as usual, practical. 'We felt it would be an injustice for a family to be deprived of its pet because the breadwinner was fighting for his country,' wrote C. Rowland Johns. Through the press and through posters, leaflets and letters written on behalf of enlisted men to their commanding officers, the League promised to help threatened families. As a result, 'over 150 dogs are receiving regular supplies of dog biscuits from the League,' Mr Johns told members at the end of 1914. In 1915 several thousand bags of similar delicacies were sent out on the League's behalf by Spratts, the dog-food manufacturer.

'In these days when the men are away,' wrote Mr Johns, 'the dog is even more appreciated than he was before. Lonely women, living in isolated spots far away from the centres of population, find in their dogs not only consolation, but also protection. Other dogs are the companions and devoted friends of children whose fathers and brothers are undergoing undreamed-of hardships for the sake of their country . . . It would be a rude hand and a cast-iron mind that would rob them of the happiness which comes from true friendship with a dog.'

Unfortunately, rude hands and cast-iron minds existed in large numbers and in some of the highest places in the land.

The 'Anti-Dog Campaign', as the League dubbed it, which began with that early advice to get rid of the family pet, really took off in 1915, when letters began appearing in the press denouncing dogs as a national menace and their owners as selfish and unpatriotic; there were proposals not just to ban all dogs in towns and cities, but to put most of them down (only working and sporting dogs were to be exempt). By 1917, with merchant ships under constant U-boat attack and food supplies at desperation-point (in the spring of that year Britain was down to a fortnight's food in reserve), the question of who should get what was on everyone's lips. Needless to say, dogs came very low on the list of priorities; there were those, indeed, who thought that, far from consuming food, they should be used to provide it. Eventually, in answer to the clamour, the Government drew up plans to destroy at least fifty per cent of the country's dog population. This would be achieved by much higher taxation, severe restrictions on breeding and the immediate destruction of all strays, who would inevitably include thousands of dogs thrown out as a direct result of the first of these measures.

The Rt Hon. A. Bonar Law. *(Mary Evans Picture Library)*

Again the League's response was immediate and effective. A deputation consisting of Lord Lambourne (the former Col. Lockwood), C. Rowland Johns and Sir Frederick Banbury went to see Bonar Law, the Chancellor of the Exchequer. The strength and

A German U-boat sinks another British freighter. *(Imperial War Museum)*

simplicity of their argument was too much for the Chancellor: he withdrew the plans in July 1917.

The League were well aware, however, that this was but a battle won. Sure enough, in the spring of 1918, when supplies of dog-food ingredients were almost exhausted, the Government refused to allow any more to be released or imported. The League had done everything possible during the preceding year to change the eating habits of dogs so that they consumed far fewer of the precious cereals that were the basis of their diet, but substitutes too were limited (in nutritional value as well as quantity) and biscuits and meal remained an essential requirement if dogs were not to be starved out of existence, something their enemies awaited with glee.

By now the Government had set up an inter-departmental committee under Hayes Fisher (later Lord Downham) to deal with the whole question of feeding and licensing. The League were invited to discuss the problem with the committee, who probably didn't appreciate what they had let themselves in for. This time Lord Lambourne and C. Rowland Johns were joined by the President, Colonel Sladen, Colonel Burn MP and R. Vaughan Gower (later Sir Robert Gower). Their argument, eloquently put, and at some length, boiled down to this: the dog must not be treated as the pariah of the animal world.

Hayes Fisher relented as quickly, if not quite as completely, as had Bonar Law before him and agreed to release a small amount of foodstuff to the dog-food manufacturers. The question of higher taxation was, as Bonar Law had already made clear, to be deferred.

Only the League's 'super-campaign' averted the threatened extermination of dogs during the war.

In the end, nothing came of it – the dog-owners' lobby, led by the League, proving to be at least as strong-willed as that of its opponents – and by 1919 the League could look back with justifiable pride on a campaign to save the dog which had been impassioned but reasonable, alert and persistent and persuasive enough to rout an opposition which had seen the war as a heaven-sent opportunity to rid the country of what they regarded as a nuisance and a menace.

'We met a violent agitation with a super-campaign,' C. Rowland Johns told members with becoming immodesty in 1919. 'Although the economic circumstances were against us, we had on our side that noble sentiment which has been awakened and kept alive by the great qualities which commend themselves to all who have ever known and loved the dog.' As one national newspaper put it, 'The dog-lovers were organised and determined; they were united.'

The League had, of course, been united over their concern for the wellbeing and safety of dogs for nearly thirty years. 'If anyone in the future shall ask for proof of our usefulness,' wrote Mr Johns, 'we may, with truth and justice, place among our list of achievements the fact that ours is "the League which saved the dogs".'

The war created many new problems, but it also exacerbated familiar ones. For the poorest dog-owners, paying the licence fee had always been difficult. Once the recruitment offices opened and the volunteers began to enlist (one million of them in 1914), it became impossible.

'A retriever to the end': from a drawing made in the trenches, 1918. *(Mary Evans Picture Library)*

Nell, a messenger dog on the Western Front: a picture that characterises the friendship often forged between dogs and the British Tommy.

A private's pay in the British army was 7s. a week, less 11d. stoppages. Living costs rose sharply as soon as the war began (food prices doubled between 1914 and 1917). How was the 7s.6d. to be paid? The League asked the Inland Revenue to waive it in the case of soldiers' and sailors' families. The Inland Revenue said it needed the money. So the League appealed once more for contributions to the Licence Fund and once more the response was magnificent. They were able to pay for 650 licences in 1915 and for over 2,000 a year later. By the end of the war, they had paid for 12,500, at a cost of £4,500, all of it raised through the Fund.

As they had before the war, the League made out the licences themselves, to make sure that they were issued only to owners genuinely anxious to keep and care for their dogs. Warmhearted and ever willing to help as they were, the League were not going to be a soft touch: the welfare of the dogs always came first. In 1916 they even proposed that the tax should become due when a dog was only two weeks old rather than after six months, with the idea of making would-be owners think twice before taking on a sweet, cuddly puppy who six months later would be chucked out as excess baggage.

That the Licence Fund was serving an even more desperate need than it did in peacetime was illustrated by the number of letters of thanks the League received from servicemen and their families, including some as grateful for the tact with which the help was given as for the sum itself. 'This is the third year I have asked you to help me keep my dog,' wrote one correspondent in 1917. 'My husband is still in France. When he writes home he always wants to know how his dog is.' A sailor's wife wrote to say that her husband bought their dog just before being taken prisoner in the North Sea in the first month of the war. 'We would like to keep her, but everything is so dear, and I have five children, but it would seem like parting with one of them to part with her.'

Those who were indifferent to such feelings took no account of the fact that at the front many men adopted local strays as pets, or were in daily contact with the hundreds of dogs used by the armies, so that they were constantly reminded of their pets at home. 'It is the dogs', wrote the *Times* correspondent from France in 1917, 'who enlist the men's sympathies more than anything else. Like frightened children, they join the ranks, nestling down by the side of the men for warmth and protection.' As Sloan and Farquar[1] put it, 'When one of them was lucky enough to become attached to a British Tommy, his future was assured.' The idea of coming home and finding that their own dog had been sent away or put down filled such men with horror. Their feelings could not be ignored, and the League took it upon themselves to make sure they were not.

The League worked to protect the interests of all dogs involved in one way or another in the war, whether at the front or in military camps at home and overseas. Shortly after the war began, for instance, they were instrumental in getting the War Office to drop the idea of using dogs to draw guns at the front. In 1916 they publicised their services at military camps in Britain, so that strays

A dog-drawn machine-gun section before the war. All the dogs were later killed in action.

[1] in *Dog and Man* by A. Sloan and A. Farquhar (Hutchinson & Co.)

who had attached themselves to the camps, feeding on scraps given to them by the troops, might be found homes, a need which became acute when the camps were broken up in 1919, leaving hundreds of dogs roaming the countryside.

Everyone had to wear gas-masks. The Belgian Front, 1915.

The League were also on hand after the war when the War Office sought help in finding good homes for the 'volunteer' dogs who had served so well on the various fronts as messengers, guard-dogs, sentries, first-aid auxiliaries – leading ambulancemen to wounded soldiers – and even (though rather less officially) as rat-catchers in the infested trenches, and whose former owners were not reclaiming them. These dogs, many of them trained at the War Dog School in Shoeburyness, Essex (within sound of the big guns, to get them used to the constant noise), had given extraordinary service. They saved an unknown number of lives through their bravery and displayed an uncanny ability to find their way across unfamiliar, featureless terrain: it was common for a dog to make its way through several miles of trenches while under intense enemy barrage to deliver a message that could not have been got through by any other means.

So diverse were the demands on the League's time and vigilance during the war that sometimes even they must have felt overwhelmed. In 1916, for example, they discovered that pets were being auctioned off on behalf of War Funds, with little or no regard for their futures. 'A strong stand has been made by the League against this abuse,' C. Rowland Johns told members. The most serious case was that of the 'Our Day' sale in support of the Red

Cross. Mr Johns went to this sale and bought fourteen dogs on the League's behalf to save them from what he knew would be mostly unpleasant fates. Some were knocked down for as little as 6d. It says much for the unswerving determination of the League that they had no hesitation in condemning such an auction despite the fact that the proceeds were going to an unimpeachable cause. A maltreated dog is a maltreated dog, war or no war.

The League even had to remind owners not to forget their dogs during air-raids. Often the poor animal was left outside when the shelter door slammed shut, to take his chances with whatever the Zeppelins or bombers cared to throw down.

Throughout the war years, the League pursued its campaigns against vivisection, chaining, cruelty and abandonment with as much vigour as ever.

In 1914 the Dogs (Protection) Bill received a second reading at last and was passed by 122 votes to 80 in the teeth of fierce opposition. But without the support of the Government, it was wrecked in committee. Once war had been declared, the Government vetoed all private members' Bills, so nothing further could be done other than to keep the subject before the public and remind them of just how many dogs and other animals were being subjected to these tortures. Home Office figures for 1916 confirmed that 612 dogs and cats were experimented on without anaesthetic in that year and a further 220 allowed to 'recover' after serious operations. In 1918 the figures were overall worse – 2,117 and 149 – but within a year they had dropped dramatically, to 174 and 66. Can it be a coincidence that the League reactivated its anti-vivisection campaign at the end of 1918, starting with a plea to members to demand support for the Bill from candidates in the December 1918 General Election?

A British airship photographed over Harwich on the day the German fleet surrendered, November 1918. Earlier in the war, similar machines designed by Count Ferdinand von Zeppelin had brought English cities their first taste of aerial bombardment. *(Imperial War Museum)*

Once more the Bill got its second reading, but once more it foundered in committee, though it did reach the report stage before its opponents (supported by almost the entire British press, clearly not made of the same stuff as its predecessors) brought it down; even so, it took a three-line Government whip to defeat it. Although the Bill failed again in 1921, Sir Frederick Banbury, still leading the fight, vowed that 'it will be introduced every session until it is passed'.

It came as a complete surprise to the League when in 1918 orders for the compulsory muzzling of dogs were issued in Devon and Cornwall. More orders followed and London was 'muzzled' early in 1919. The reason? The League had its own ideas. As C. Rowland Johns put it in his annual report for that year, 'By a strange coincidence, at the time when the Dogs (Protection) Bill was before

Learning to cope under rifle fire: army dogs training for war service.

Parliament, a great scare arose about rabies . . . The incontrovertible truth [is] that no person in this country had suffered from hydrophobia as a result of being bitten by a dog.' It was another crisis for the League to deal with amid its attempts to find homes for war dogs and the swollen army of strays, as well as coping with all its other work. There was a rush for muzzles and owners faced the absurd risk of being prosecuted for breaching the regulations by the very act of taking their dogs out in search of one. The League promised to protect anyone so prosecuted and the authorities were sensible enough not to put them to the test.

Not only were dogs forcibly muzzled, but their movements, and therefore those of their owners, were severely restricted by a rule which said that if a dog was moved from one district to another it would have to be quarantined for six months. While fighting such examples of 'overkill' with some success (they had the six months reduced to one), the League pressed for the total abolition of muzzling as an unnecessary reaction to a very small problem. For all their efforts, however, muzzling did not end until early 1922, after three-and-a-half years of hardship for dogs, inconvenience and expense for their owners (and sometimes the vilification of their neighbours) and for the League a long struggle to counter the hysteria those rabies reports in 1918 had generated.

Typically, their first act after the last order was lifted was to ask the Government to tell the railway companies that it was no longer necessary for dogs to travel in guards' vans. It was a bye-law of most of the companies that dogs should not travel with passengers but

Turc, from the famous St Bernard Hospice in the Swiss Alps, with a local priest. Turc had already rescued thirty-two people trapped on the mountains by the time this picture was taken in 1920.

until the rabies scares most had let this pass. The companies were glad to restore the dog to its accustomed place, not least because during those three-and-a-half years many owners had stopped using the trains altogether rather than be separated from their pets. As Mr Johns put it in the *Dogs' Bulletin*, 'We believe that, in the face of road competition, the railways companies will find it profitable to keep upon amicable terms with dog-owners.'

The *Dogs' Bulletin*, incidentally, began life in September 1920. It was sent free to subscribers, some of whom sent 2s. a year to cover printing and postage costs. From these modest beginnings it blossomed and appeared regularly for the next thirty years. Subscribers came from outside the League to swell the circulation, such groups as Young Farmers' Clubs becoming regular readers, which was encouraging, since country dogs were all too often treated as cruelly as their urban brothers: the life at the end of a chain endured by Edmund Blunden's farm-dog in Flanders (*see* p. 39) was just as common on this side of the Channel.

An exclusive diet of stories of cruelty to dogs would have been hard for anyone to take and the League, ever optimistic about man's feelings for dogs despite so much evidence to the contrary, were always keen to publicise stories of extraordinary courage on behalf of dogs by people of all ages. Particularly noble, perhaps, was the effort of the young policeman near Cardiff in 1914 who, lowered by his companions forty feet down a cliff-face to rescue a dog trapped on a ledge, found what appeared to be a rather ungrateful animal waiting for him. Every time he reached out for it with one hand, hanging on for dear life with the other, the dog scampered to the other side of the ledge. We may safely assume that conversation between them became rather strained. Eventually the poor policeman had to be hauled up, exhausted from his efforts, to be replaced by a colleague, who managed to persuade the cheery beast that the alternative to rescue was not something a dog of such spirit should contemplate.

There were, as ever, many dog heroes, warning households of danger, chasing burglars and making some remarkable rescues of their own. Jack, a dog of unnamed breed, rescued no fewer than four children on separate occasions from a river near his home, pulling them to the bank and barking until help came. Tearie, a Midlothian retriever, saved his master's small daughter by pulling her from a trap behind a bolting pony just before it overturned.

Such stories were good for dogs and good for the League. It did their cause no harm to be associated with a celebrity from time to time, and if that celebrity was himself a dog, so much the better.

Two of their biggest 'star turns' during this period were Bobs (another one) and Onkie. One is a story with a happy ending, the other not, but both showed the League at its fighting best.

Bobs, the pet of a London schoolgirl, was picked up one day in 1919 without a muzzle (muzzling orders had only just been introduced). Described by the police as vicious and uncontrollable, he was sentenced by the local magistrate to be put down. Immediate execution was averted by a bunch of schoolchildren, who swept Bobs up and bore him away to his nearby home, which the police proceeded to besiege for two days, demanding him back 'but failing to secure possession of him', as the 1919 annual report drily put it.

The League took up Bobs' case, both for its own sake and because it seemed to them to reflect the increasingly unreasonable official attitude towards dogs since the rabies scare. They appealed against the death sentence at Clerkenwell court, having in the meantime turned Bobs into a national hero and collected 20,000 signatures supporting his release. 'A motor char-a-banc of witnesses for the defence drove to the Court,' wrote C. Rowland Johns, 'with Bobs occupying the front seat and looking complacently at the forty or more photographers and cinema operators who assembled to secure pictures of the event.' If every dog has his day, this was surely Bobs'.

Mr Curtis Bennett KC appeared for the League and, following classic courtroom procedure, called as his main defence witness the accused. Bobs was impeccable throughout, sitting quietly on the bench in front of the magistrate, who was so completely disarmed that he quashed the conviction without further ado. 'The greatest dog drama in history,' as one London paper called it, was over. Bobs

Apologies for the poor quality of this and the following illustration, but both are from unique 'on-the-spot' photographs (taken by the *Daily Mail*) of the famous Bobs at the time of his 'trial'. Here Bobs is protected by a posse of children, including those who rescued him from his first court appearance . . .

. . . and here Bobs is seen at the appeal court, surrounded by an even more imposing posse of lawyers.

was reunited with his mistress and the League had once again done its stuff – 'a successful effort to secure common justice,' as Mr Johns called it, '[which] typifies the spirit which animates your League.'

Onkie was a fox terrier condemned to death by magistrates at Kingston, Surrey, in 1920. The League first appealed to the quarter sessions and ultimately to the Home Secretary himself, but to no avail. 'Probably since the first association of dogs with man,' wrote the *Bulletin*, 'no more persistent efforts have been made to save the life of a single dog . . .' The owners did have one alternative offered to them: they could keep the dog provided they paid a fine of £1 every day for the rest of his life. It was an impossible burden and Onkie was put to sleep on the twelfth day of Christmas, 1921, leaving the League determined to see the laws involved changed.

Public interest in Bobs and Onkie – and others – brought in further support for the League, help which was very welcome, for the cost of such actions was high and money was constantly needed for every branch of their activities. Of these, none was more needy than the Stray Dogs' Fund as the League fought against the growing tide of abandoned dogs. Fortunately – or rather, through forethought and hard work – they had one important development on their side.

In 1914 it was C. Rowland Johns himself who provided the inspiration behind a move to get all the animal welfare organisations working together to rescue strays. He called it the 'Save the Dog' campaign and it was the first time anyone had attempted to coordinate the efforts of the various groups and in particular to publicise all dog shelters and animal homes, regardless of which group ran them, through a series of united campaigns.

By 1917 the League had persuaded the authorities in London to print on the back of every new dog licence a list of all the shelters available in the capital, of which only the one in Fulham was run exclusively by the League. In Liverpool a similar scheme drew attention to the League's Edge Lane home, which promised to collect unwanted dogs for a 1s. fee. The idea spread and more and more strays were brought to shelters instead of being kicked out. The Fulham shelter doubled its intake in a year and by 1921 the Metropolitan Police were able to report a fifty per cent drop in the number of strays on the streets of London as compared with five years before.

All this put an enormous strain on the Stray Dogs' Fund, but members and donors rallied round as heroically as ever. 'The "Save the Dog" campaign', wrote C. Rowland Johns in 1918, 'is a great movement forward . . . The systematic and efficient handling of a grave problem has begun.' The League opened four more of its own shelters in the capital in 1918, though this wasn't an easy undertaking: the shelters had to be close enough to centres of population to encourage people to use them yet, paradoxically, far enough away not to be a public nuisance.

Another League medal-winner: George Green, of Pwllheli, North Wales, with the dog he saved from drowning.

> [I] watched the company depart down the muddy by-road past the ovens and tents in a depressed mood, nor was I alone in my regret. The smelly little farmyard dog, who had been taken off his chain in the night by our humanitarians, and walked out into a liberty which he could scarcely remember since his puppy days, also gazed, and hung a mournful head.
>
> – from *Undertones of War*, by Edmund Blunden

It may be self-indulgent to imagine that Edmund Blunden's humanitarians were influenced by the National Canine Defence League's ceaseless campaigns against chaining. Yet they were campaigns on some scale, with over 200,000 leaflets distributed in a typical year and widespread postering with the help of the police, the Salvation Army and other groups, all supported by a regular bombardment of letters to, and well-placed stories in, the newspapers; and the League had been campaigning thus for twenty years or more. Perhaps those departing soldiers would have released their forlorn little friend anyway, yet had the League known of the story at the time they would surely have been heartened by it.

Too many owners seemed not to realise how cruel it was to deprive dogs of the freedom they craved – or didn't care. 'There are many people', wrote C. Rowland Johns, 'who would chain even their children to a tree-trunk, only that they are afraid of the criticisms of their associates.'

The League wasn't afraid to challenge an owner in court if necessary. In 1916 they discovered a terrier who had been chained to a fence for seven weeks while its owner was away. They took the dog into care, told the owner they had no intention of returning it to him and dared him to take the case to law. He declined the challenge. Only rarely did a case actually reach the courts: the League's favoured method was not to apply the heavy hand, but to appeal to reason. It was usually enough to talk to an owner, who either mended his ways or handed his dog over to the League.

Choclat *(in close-up, below)*, a performing dog handed over to the League after the successful prosecution of his owner for cruelty, is seen performing the sort of trick to which many dog lovers objected.

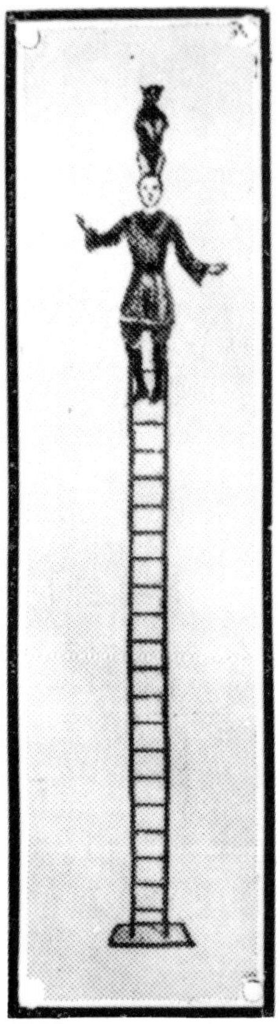

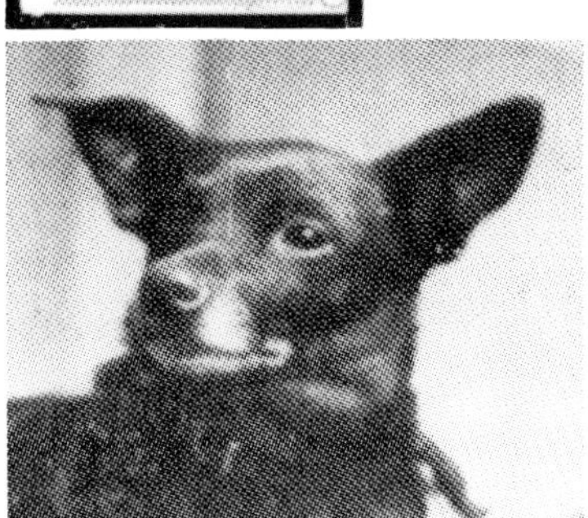

'An old-established practice is not swept away like chaff before the wind,' warned C. Rowland Johns in 1920, perhaps thinking particularly of farm-dogs, for the problem, acute anyway in rural districts, was made worse by the tax exemptions allowed to farmers and others who could show that theirs were working dogs. The League persuaded one or two magistrates to withhold exemptions where dogs were kept constantly chained. They also considered introducing an anti-chaining Bill in Parliament, but in fact existing legislation already made chaining an offence. It was getting magistrates to apply the law that was the difficulty.

At last, in 1921, and after careful preparation, the League did take a case to court, in Tower Bridge, London, and were fully vindicated when the magistrate found unequivocally in their favour and condemned the practice as *in itself* a criminal offence. The League made a point of selecting an owner who could afford to defend himself. They wanted a cast-iron verdict, one which would carry real weight with other magistrates. They were duly rewarded. They could now say, 'Prolonged chaining is illegal,' and know that this meant exactly what it said and that penalties would be exacted for ignoring it.

Although the campaign against the abuse of performing dogs had previously gone well, the League had no reason to be complacent. In 1914 the showmen came up with the crafty idea of a form of self-regulation, by which licences would be granted for the use of animals where no cruelty was observed at a rehearsal watched by an inspector. The League soon saw off that one. Another success was the removal from its showman-owner of a dog, Choclat, who had been kept in a tiny cardboard box for six weeks, let out only for performances. The owner was taken to court under the Forfeit Clause of the Protection of Animals Act 1911. The Drury Lane Theatre was prosecuted for neglecting several sick dogs performing there. And the League pointed out an anomaly in the quarantine laws, which allowed performing dogs to enter the country with impunity, giving privileges to particularly callous owners.

Dogs suffered terribly learning tricks such as this to 'entertain' music-hall audiences. The League were among the first to condemn such displays. *(Mary Evans Picture Library)*

By the end of 1919 the League had persuaded one major music-hall chain not to book any performing-animal acts and in 1921 the Performing Animals Bill was lost only on its third reading, though a select committee was given the task of looking into the whole business.

As Samuel James, owner of the Lyric Theatre, Hammersmith, told the League in a letter to the *Bulletin*: 'I have had fifteen theatres [and] music halls. I can assure you that all animal stage acts are produced by cruelty. No lover of dumb animals should ever let one penny of his money go into the pockets of the trainer.'

A case which caused special revulsion was that of the Anglo-American Exhibition at Shepherds Bush in 1914, when a troop of Red Indians planned to kill and eat a number of dogs on stage. No doubt they saw this as a way of enlightening the English public about their traditional ways. The League were quick to enlighten them in turn about the Englishman's love of dogs and the intended victims were saved.

In October 1914 the Board of Agriculture announced that the quarantine period for imported dogs was to be reduced forthwith

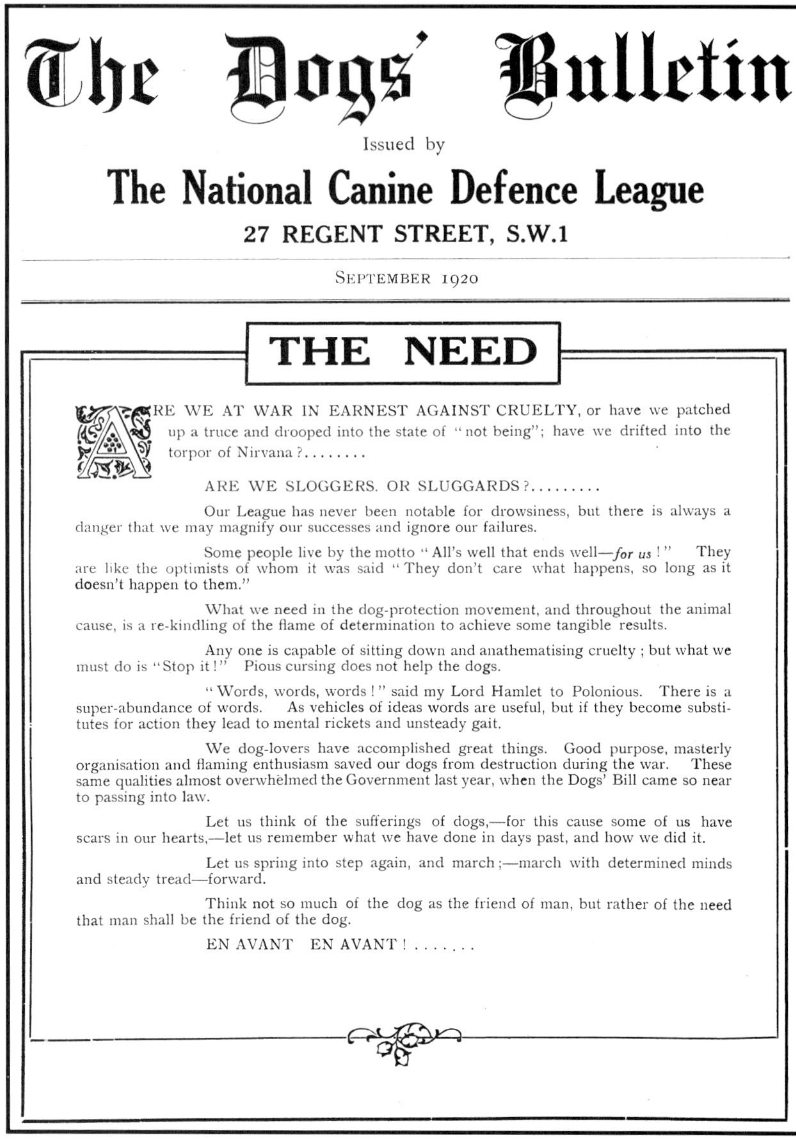

The Dogs' Bulletin

Issued by

The National Canine Defence League

27 REGENT STREET, S.W.1

SEPTEMBER 1920

THE NEED

ARE WE AT WAR IN EARNEST AGAINST CRUELTY, or have we patched up a truce and drooped into the state of "not being"; have we drifted into the torpor of Nirvana?........

ARE WE SLOGGERS, OR SLUGGARDS?.........

Our League has never been notable for drowsiness, but there is always a danger that we may magnify our successes and ignore our failures.

Some people live by the motto "All's well that ends well—*for us*!" They are like the optimists of whom it was said "They don't care what happens, so long as it doesn't happen to them."

What we need in the dog-protection movement, and throughout the animal cause, is a re-kindling of the flame of determination to achieve some tangible results.

Any one is capable of sitting down and anathematising cruelty; but what we must do is "Stop it!" Pious cursing does not help the dogs.

"Words, words, words!" said my Lord Hamlet to Polonious. There is a super-abundance of words. As vehicles of ideas words are useful, but if they become substitutes for action they lead to mental rickets and unsteady gait.

We dog-lovers have accomplished great things. Good purpose, masterly organisation and flaming enthusiasm saved our dogs from destruction during the war. These same qualities almost overwhelmed the Government last year, when the Dogs' Bill came so near to passing into law.

Let us think of the sufferings of dogs,—for this cause some of us have scars in our hearts,—let us remember what we have done in days past, and how we did it.

Let us spring into step again, and march;—march with determined minds and steady tread—forward.

Think not so much of the dog as the friend of man, but rather of the need that man shall be the friend of the dog.

EN AVANT EN AVANT! ....

The front cover of the first issue of the *Dogs' Bulletin*.

from six months to four and that, where it could be proved that dogs on ships which had called only briefly at foreign ports on their way to Britain had not been landed or come into contact with local animals, they would be exempt from quarantine altogether.

Who was it who persuaded the Board to take these long-overdue measures? 'We never rested' might be a good motto for the League. Nothing concerning the welfare of dogs escaped their attention. For example, they sought the help of vets in a campaign to persuade owners to provide their sick and injured dogs with proper medical care. As ever, people preferred to 'let nature take its course', as in the case of the Devon farmer's dog injured in a gin-trap. For five months he was allowed to wander around, hobbling and in obvious pain, before being found by a stranger and taken to a vet. The farmer was fined, the dog recovered.

Alternatively, owners reluctant to pay veterinary fees would try applying their own hazy notions of animal first aid, more often than not making things worse. 'There is a great deal too much amateur doctoring of dogs,' observed the League. They might have added that the gin-trap victim was lucky in one respect: many injured and sick dogs were simply disposed of by their owners in that variety of unspeakable ways with which the League was all too familiar. (One pair of unwanted terrier pups were thrown alive into a furnace.)

Occasionally the League's ideas were perhaps a little too ambitious. One such was the plan to open squares in towns and cities for the early-morning recreation of dogs. They commissioned a 'feasibility study'; on receiving it they issued the briefest of statements: 'For the time being it has been thought better not to incur further expense in this direction.'

'The dog is the best-treated animal in Britain,' wrote someone to the *Bulletin* in 1920 as a reason for not joining the League.

'If we had been inclined to believe that dogs had already achieved paradise,' C. Rowland Johns wrote in response, 'we should have had a rude blow the other day at Ealing, when we prosecuted a man for kicking a dog so hard that the dog died half an hour later. . . . The defendant admitted the kicking: he declared that he did it because his wife was screaming and was in a delicate state of health. The dog was not attacking her or him.'

Reproduced opposite is the *Bulletin*'s front-page editorial for its first issue. Anyone who may have entertained doubts about the League's continuing determination to conquer evil could not still have had them after reading this. *En avant* indeed.

By the end of 1920, the postwar economic boom was already coming to an end and hard times clearly lay ahead. The League appealed to members and donors for help to strengthen their funds, particularly the Licence Fund. They knew that demands on this and indeed all their resources would grow irresistibly as the threat of mass unemployment began to cast its shadow over the short-lived days of postwar euphoria.

. . . The poor dog, in life the firmest friend,
The first to welcome, foremost to defend;
Whose honest heart is still his master's own;
Who labours, fights, lives, breathes for him alone.

Lord Byron

3 New clinics, fresh crises

Between the wars, 1922–1939

Within four years of the Armistice, there were over two million unemployed in Britain, and 'the League that saved the dogs' found itself having to save a lot of them all over again.

As they had anticipated, demand for help from the Licence Fund soared. In 1923 they paid for over 3,500 licences, in 1927 (by which time they had moved offices to Victoria Street, handily placed for the Houses of Parliament) for a record 4,600. Although the main crisis had passed by the early thirties, even in 1938 they were answering pleas from nearly 1,500 desperate owners.

A pensioner wrote in 1934: 'I am 62 years of age, 32 years a complete cripple . . . my income is 8s. 5d. a week. It takes 3s. 3d. in firing, 2s. 6d. rent, so I have not much left. My dog is my only pal, as I live by myself in a rather isolated spot.' One dog in Sussex was the lucky recipient of a licence for life, the gift of a neighbour who took pity on its poverty-stricken owner.

Another successful campaign by the League: providing free drinking water for dogs in east London in the 1930s.

'If those who give to the Fund could only be personal witnesses of the joy which the poor owners of dogs feel when the licences arrive from the League,' C. Rowland Johns wrote, 'they would feel amply repaid.' Donors hardly needed such encouragement. 'I am enclosing £1 2s. 6d. (three dog licences),' wrote one, 'as I know what it means to part with a beloved pet. . . .'

The League pressed for a change in the licensing laws. 'If dogs could understand calendars, many of them would now be enduring anxious days,' said the *Bulletin* in February 1922. 'On the 1st of January the poorest dog-owners are at their wits' end to find food not only for their dogs but for themselves. It is unfair to submit their affection for their dogs to so great a trial by asking them to find [7s. 6d.] in the depths of winter.' They tried to persuade the Government to change the licence date to the summer months, when work was easier to find, or to start the licence year from the date of issue of each licence. Predictably, the local authorities, who were responsible for collecting the tax, didn't find the extra paperwork likely to be involved to their fancy and turned the idea down.

The League now asked applicants to pay the first 2s. 6d. of the tax if they possibly could. In this way, they argued, they could spread their help more widely. They also ran random checks on claims and got the police to follow up suspicious applications. One miscreant ended up paying for the equivalent of three licences, in the form of a fine, instead of the one he had tried to get for nothing.

The Licence Fund had struck a chord among dog-lovers from its inception in 1910 and each year donations arrived at the League's headquarters in a modest but steady stream; this was due in no small measure to the support it received from the press, in particular the *Daily Mirror*, who in 1923 gave the Fund a cheque for £567, raised entirely by their readers. So generous were donors that other charities, when their own resources had been depleted, passed deserving cases on to the League.

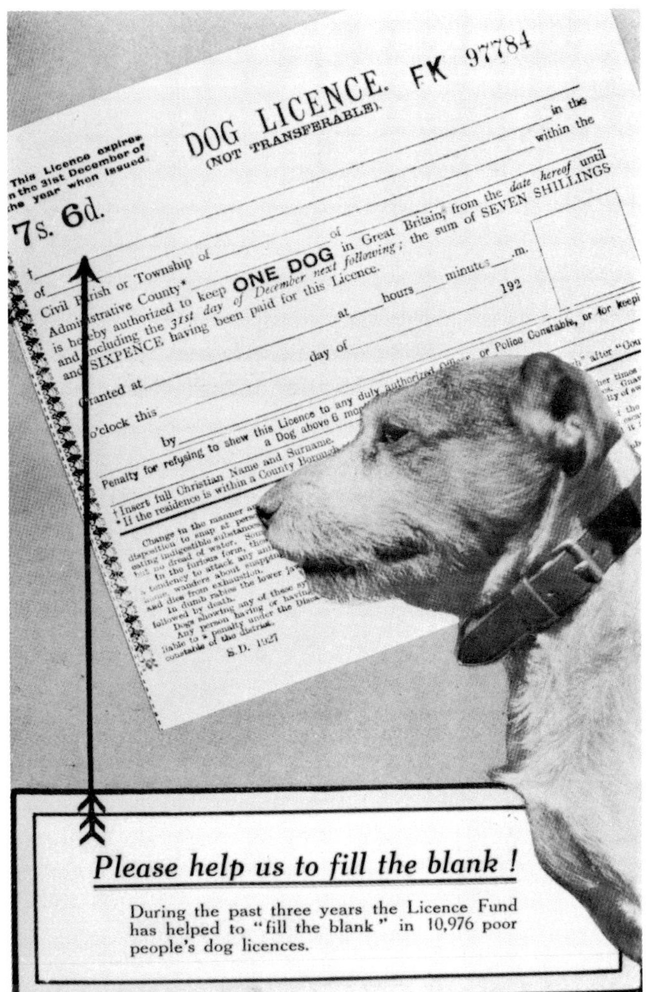

An appeal for cash to swell the much-in-demand Licence Fund, 1930.

Sitting in slightly awkward juxtaposition to their determination to enable all dog-lovers to keep their pets was the League's anxiety about the speed with which the dog population was growing. In 1924 there were a million more dogs in Britain than there had been twenty years before. The League knew that something had to be done, for along with the rise in ownership went, as an inevitable concomitant, an increase in the number of abandoned and stray dogs, just when it had seemed that this problem might be under control.

Various solutions were suggested. One was increasing the licence fee (which in several European countries was four times higher than in Britain), ensuring that only those who could afford to look after a dog properly bought one in the first place.

Given their principles, the League had to reject this idea, for the very reason that made it so attractive – its prohibitiveness – just as in 1930 they objected to a Government plan to introduce a phased tax (£1 for the first dog up to £8 for the fourth, and so on), reminding the Chancellor, Philip Snowden, that such an idea had been floated during the war, 'but the League prevented it from being put into operation . . .'

When C. Rowland Johns went on holiday to Norway, he hardly saw a dog at all – three in three days in the capital, Oslo. The reason was simple: the dog tax was anything from £2 10s. to £5, depending on the breed. Introducing such swingeing taxes into Britain might have usefully diminished the purchase of puppies, but it would also have led to the wholesale abandonment or destruction of older dogs, something the League could not countenance.

As the arguments over the licence raged, the dog population grew greater by the day, and the stray problem correspondingly worse.

A League member suggested that the tax, far from being raised, should be lowered to 5s. This, he claimed, would reduce the incidence of kicked-out dogs overnight; as for the Treasury's lost income, they could make this up by taxing the even greater cat population. C. Rowland Johns gave his backing, suggesting that the proceeds (2s. 6d. per cat would be about right, in his view) should all go to animal welfare societies, thus ensuring that the money went where it was most needed, as was the case in America with an idea the League had been trying to get made law in Britain for many years – tax discs on dog-collars.

In New York, where income from the disc went entirely to the American SPCA, the shape of the disc changed annually, so that defaulting owners could be spotted quickly; and each disc, which was printed by the tax authorities themselves, carried the number of the equivalent licence, together with the owner's name and address. This last requirement, such an obvious way to reunite lost dogs with their owners, did not become law in this country until 1930, with the Control of Dogs Order. Prior to that it had been left to the discretion of local authorities.

The League paid for over 3,000 licences in 1924 alone. This pet was clearly determined to ensure that his owner did the right thing.

Another American concept of which the League approved was the discount tax: you paid \$2 in the first year and \$1 each year thereafter, provided you renewed your licence in time. Some bright spark even suggested that dogs should be taxed by size, to which the League gently replied that 'unfortunately . . . a dog's appetite, like his master's, is by no means in strict ratio to his avoir-dupois'. The League themselves proposed an instalment plan for poorer owners, though they still championed the proposal that taxation should start much earlier – at six weeks, they now suggested – to discourage irresponsible ownership.

None of these ideas was taken up by the authorities in Britain – though they did agree to notify the League of any cases of hardship before taking anyone to court, a small but important concession – and by 1936 the League were frustrated enough to propose open mutiny.

'WHY PAY THE DOG TAX?' ran a *Bulletin* headline. 'The vast sum of £1,000,000 is just taken from dog-owners without a "thank-you" and goes to relieve local rates.' The system was so well established that no one thought to question it. 'Yet what an outcry there would be if motorists had no new roads paid for out of motor-taxation! How radio-listeners would squeal if they were not given more and/or better programmes as the "wireless" tax receipts increase!'

> We note that, in those cities where the police and local Dogs' Homes are not progressive enough to avail themselves of the League's cooperation, the statistics show an increase in the number of stray dogs which are picked up by the police, and we observe that, where our posters are well shown, and our leaflets

The police cooperated closely with charities like the League in saving strays.

> generously distributed, and the Dogs' Homes keep their doors open for dogs which are brought in direct by their owners, the number of strays is in decline.

Thus spake the League in 1923, and it was no more than the truth. Their publicity and propaganda machine – C. Rowland Johns – worked tirelessly through articles and letters to the press, leaflets, posters, lantern lectures, school visits and, later, cinema films like *Lucky Dogs – and Others, A Dog's Day* and *Let Dogs Delight* to bring home the message that dogs deserved both care and respect, which they would reward with a love and devotion few men could surpass.

Indeed, 'in some cases a dog actually has a higher concept of certain moral obligations than its master,' wrote the eminent trainer/breeder Col. Edwin Richardson, in the 1920s.[1] 'You may find a dog which under no circumstances will betray a trust, while its master may continually do so . . . A dog is frequently forgiving and loving, it is joyous and happy and it can also die of grief. How many people can we describe thus?'

Yet so often this simple faith in their master's honour was rewarded with indifference and rejection. The Depression brought with it, unsurprisingly, a great increase in the number of dogs thrown out. Rescuing, caring for and, where possible, finding new homes for this itinerant army of abandoned pets was a daunting task. The League's London shelters dealt with 1,500 strays in 1924, a large number of them having to be put down.

'The shelter side of our work is a difficult one to write about,' C. Rowland Johns told members. 'No one can take pleasure in accelerating the deaths of faithful and loving dogs and the scenes at a Shelter are too sad to be pictured in words. Recently, in one afternoon, forty-two dogs were brought to the Hackney-road shelter [and destroyed] . . . [poor people's dogs] are the canine equivalent to the "submerged tenth" . . .'

The shelter side of the League's work was also a difficult one to run, for not only was there the ever-present problem of finding the right premises – they had to be out of the way yet accessible – but getting the funds to keep them going was an uphill struggle, as the Gerrards Cross, Buckinghamshire, shelter found in 1925 when it had to beg for money through the *Bulletin*, local appeals having failed to come up with enough to keep it going. (Shelters tried to be self-supporting.)

As for the centres, their secretaries were to the League 'what outposts are to an army', keeping a sharp eye on what the enemies of dogs were up to and often able to deal with local skirmishes themselves. Their work, too, was made more difficult by the problem of

[1] in *Forty Years With Dogs* (Hutchinson & Co., 1920)

finding suitable premises, in which connection the League had a major stroke of luck in 1926 when they came into possession of a property which was to become famous in their history – the Hampton Home, in Middlesex, a house and two acres of grounds presented to them by a benefactor as 'a refuge for unwanted, homeless and sick dogs'. It had the advantage of being well away from densely populated areas and thus the complaints of neighbours, although the rapid development of suburban west London in the 1930s was soon to make it a lot less isolated.

The Hampton Home in 1932.

Hampton was to become a vital arm of the League, renowned for its veterinary facilities, the needs of which prompted the League to obtain its first-ever motor ambulance in 1926.

Still fighting for *the* Bill: an appeal on the front of the *Bulletin* in 1927.

Please write a

Personal Letter

— to your —

Member of Parliament

asking him to vote for the

PROTECTION OF DOGS' BILL

which would

Exempt Dogs from Painful Experiments.

For a change, legislation came to the rescue of strays to a generous degree during this period. Before the Control of Dogs Order of 1930, with its universal enforcement of dog-collar regulations, the Dogs (Amendment) Act of 1928 made it an offence to find a stray and not to endeavour either to trace the owner or to deliver it up to the police (though the maximum penalty was only £2).

Although Lord Lambourne died in 1929, depriving the League of one of its most influential advocates, League Chairman Sir Robert Gower remained a formidable Parliamentary presence and in 1938 steered through the Dogs (Amendment) Act, which provided time for appeal where destruction orders had been given against 'dangerous' dogs. A dog could be deemed 'dangerous' if it strayed once into, say, a chicken-coop, so the new law provided a welcome buffer between sentence and execution, which otherwise would have been immediate.

The League had less success with the Dogs and Cats Bill, under which the authorities would be empowered to go into laboratories and search for lost or stolen dogs and cats, and were again frustrated over *the* Bill, the Dogs (Protection) Bill.

. . . And eight years later, another no-nonsense poster.

In 1927, just when 'possibly [the Bill] had come to be regarded as a ghostly manifestation rather than a living force' after three moribund years, revelations about the trade between dog-thieves and vivisectors revived public interest in it; support from the RSPCA seemed particularly to alarm the Bill's opponents, who fought successfully to persuade them to withdraw an intended petition to Parliament.

Having achieved this, the anti-dog lobby turned their full attention to the League, whom they rightly saw as the main enemy. Led by the British Medical Association, who had a Bill of their own in mind which would permit the use of strays and stolen dogs in laboratories if they had not been claimed by their owners within the statutory seven days (thus superseding the 1906 Act, which expressly forbade such use), the League's opponents opened their campaign in April 1927 at a special conference 'to combat the League's propaganda'.

'The National Canine Defence League', said the *Bulletin* that month, 'does not complain if, while hunting lions, it sustains some scratches,' mixing its metaphors to some effect by adding that 'the battle-fleet of the BMA is the effective fighting force of the most highly organised and most strictly disciplined professional union in the world . . . they mean business. And that business is to kill the Dogs (Protection) Bill.'

The League took over the RSPCA's thwarted petition and within three months were able to present 300,000 signatures to Parliament. Despite the BMA's best efforts, the Bill reached its second reading before once again being defeated. It was further than the BMA's Bill ever got.

For so many strays, being rescued by the League was the best birthday present they could wish for.

DURING 1931

The

National Canine Defence League

Gave Treatment at its Clinics to

62,165

Sick and Injured Animals

3,492

Licences were provided for poor people's dogs

Our Veterinary Ticket Scheme also provided treatment for a large number of dogs

THINK OF THE VALUE

of this practical side of our widespread activities

Part of an appeal to members to support the League's various activities, which ate into funds at an alarming rate.

The League had always been able to rely on police help in publicising their numerous campaigns, so it was with some care that they tackled the police themselves on the subject of the housing of strays at police stations, where all too often facilities were inadequate. After the 1928 Act pressure on police kennels became even greater, so improvements were a matter of urgency.

The League wrote to the Home Office, pointing out that in London the dog licence brought in fifty-three times as much as the costs incurred in caring for stray dogs, to which Home Secretary Herbert Samuel replied that the will to help was certainly there: the police were experimenting with new kennel designs, for instance, but they were governed by what their local authorities allocated them in the way of money; the League promptly urged members to tackle their town halls if they thought that strays were not being properly looked after.

By the early thirties the League could write once more about a real reduction in the number of strays, despite the huge increase in ownership. (There were now estimated to be well over four million dogs in Britain.)

They put the improvement down to four things: 'the provision of receiving-places [for] unwanted dogs . . . the help which is given to poor people in regard to licences . . . the greater consideration which is being given to dogs . . . [and] the educational work which has pointed out the sufferings of dogs turned adrift . . .'

In all these avenues of progress, C. Rowland Johns told members, 'your League has been the pioneer'. Posters attacking the kicking-out of unwanted dogs appeared on 8,000 police noticeboards and in 2,000 schools in the London area alone during the winter of 1937, a typical year in the League's continuing struggle against behaviour for which by then there was no excuse, for there were plenty of shelters, homes and clinics to which unwanted dogs could be taken.

The League continued to open centres all over Britain, including the Sussex Home for Dogs and Cats at Brighton (where they had always had a very active branch), which they bought in 1938; but one of their most significant developments after the Great War was the establishment of their own clinics to provide expert veterinary treatment for poor people's dogs. The pioneer was the Bethnal Green clinic in London, which opened in February 1926. On their opening day they treated three dogs; within six weeks they were dealing with over fifty a day. The newly acquired Hampton Home was swiftly transformed into a clinic and one was also opened in Wandsworth, south London.

Treatment was given free of charge to those who couldn't afford to pay. Appealing for funds, C. Rowland Johns said that the hope was that the clinics 'will radiate a beneficent influence in those

A boot to mend a fractured leg, devised by staff at the Hackney clinic just before the Second World War.

districts in which they are established, and that they will become places to which all those in difficulties about their dogs, even when they are not sick or injured, will come.' A year later the South London Canine Clinic opened at Camberwell and here the League openly welcomed animals other than dogs, a policy which was to become universal at all their clinics; after all, if you were a qualified vet and someone brought in a cat with a needle stuck in its mouth, how could you turn it away on the grounds that you only dealt with dogs?

In 1929 the League opened a clinic in Croydon, Surrey ('bus no. 78 passes the door'), which incorporated two 'electrocuting machines', sometimes also called 'electric kennels', one for small animals and puppies, the other for full-size dogs. Each carried 2,000 volts 'and does its work painlessly, cleanly and silently . . . the dog is unconscious in *less than the thousandth part of a second*'. These lethal chambers were eventually taken up by many other veterinary institutions around the country and given official recognition by the report of the National Veterinary Medical Association Special Committee on Small Animal Euthanasia in 1937. Initially, they cost £65 to install 'but the running costs are small' (not least because the staff's main aim was always to save lives, not take them: they were often able to dissuade owners from having their pets put down).

In 1930 more clinics were opened, in Fulham and Camden Town, followed two years later by others in Lisson Grove, near Regent's Park, and in Teddington, Middlesex. The Cambridge Road, Hackney, clinic (to which the League had been forced to move the original Bethnal Green clinic in 1929) was itself replaced by larger premises nearby in 1934, as the Cambridge Road site was now too small to cope with demand. In 1937 a clinic was opened in Wealdstone, Middlesex.

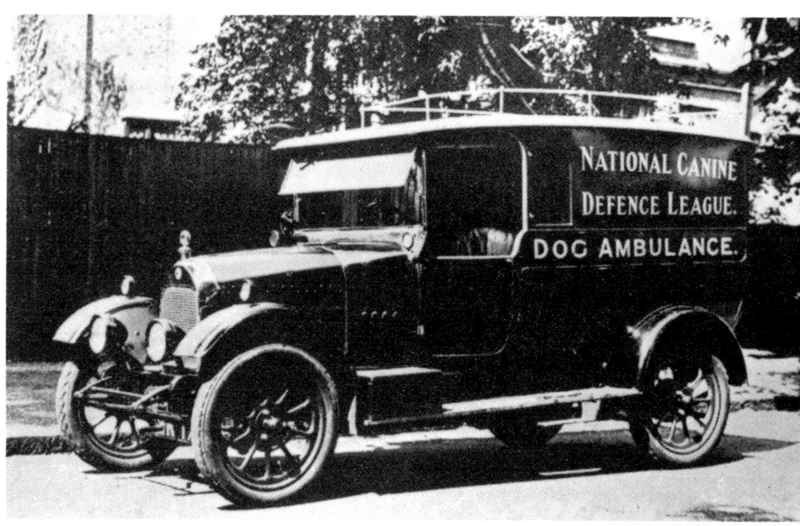

The League's first dog ambulance, purchased in 1926.

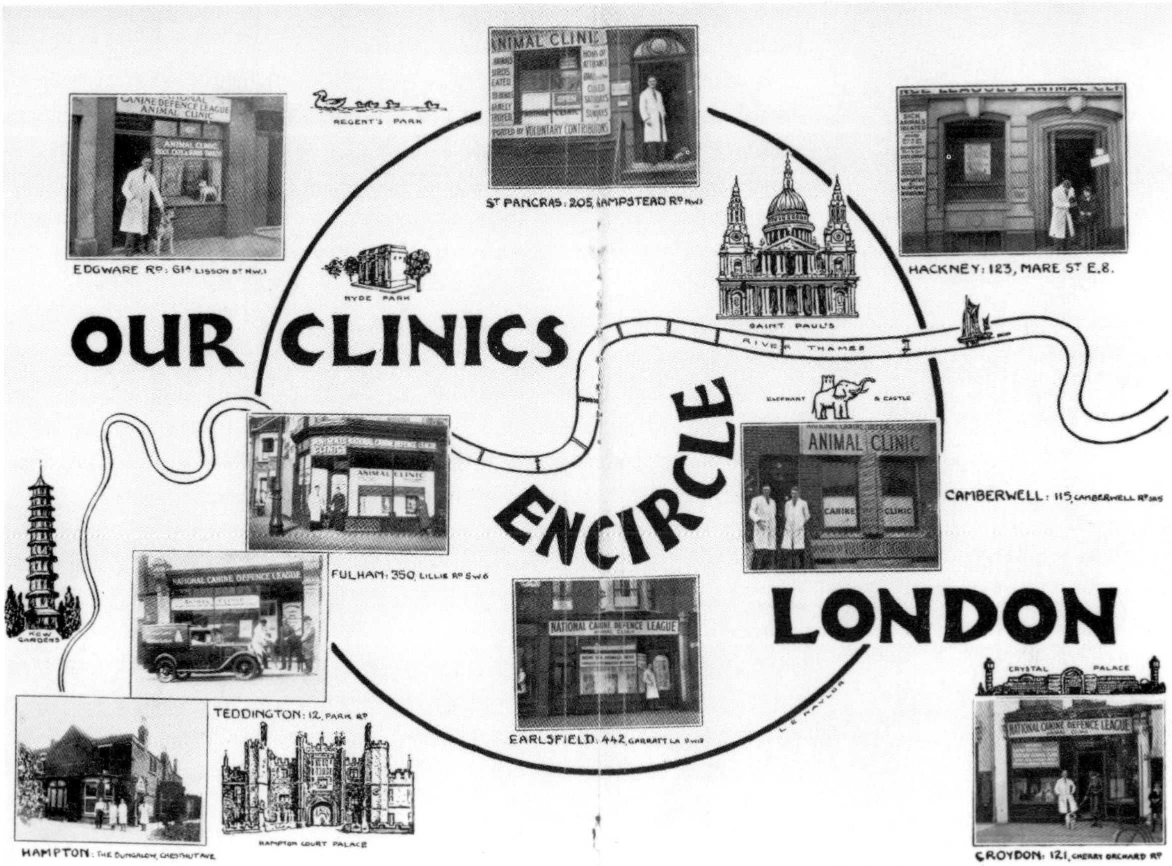

A healthy picture for the capital, 1935.

By the end of 1939 the League's clinics in and around London, now nine in number, were dealing with over 80,000 animal patients a year, from dogs to tortoises, snakes to rabbits – and, as backyard poultry became popular at the start of the Second World War, with a great many chickens, ducks and other birds, too.

Even before they launched their own clinics, the League had taken steps to help poorer owners to get proper veterinary treatment for their pets through the 'Help the Dogs' veterinary ticket scheme, inaugurated at the beginning of 1922. Under this, subscribers to the League each received a book of tickets which they could either use themselves or pass on to other owners who could not afford veterinary fees. The ticket was given to the vet in lieu of payment and he passed it on to the League with his invoice for settlement (often a much reduced bill, or even no bill at all, as a mark of his support for the scheme).

An enormous amount of suffering was saved by this simple innovation; until the ticket scheme came along, it was not unknown for a dog to be in pain for many months before its owner either would or

Selling stamps produced a small but steady income.

could do anything to help it. The new scheme was both a financial boon and an incentive to take action.

Local police cooperated by keeping books of tickets which owners could apply for; and perhaps the scheme's greatest virtue was that it reached into the most remote corners of the country in a way in which the clinics could not.

'I think it is the best thing that has ever been done for animals up to now,' wrote one League member. Its only limitation was that it had to be reserved for dogs: the available funds simply did not allow it to be used for other animals.

It will be clear from all these signs of growing activity that the League's financial position was a lot healthier by the beginning of the twenties than it had been a decade before. But life was far from easy. In 1922 assets totalled less than £15,000. By 1929 sound investment had trebled this figure and by 1938 it had more than doubled again, to £95,000. Subscriptions played only a small part in this, legacies having become a gratifyingly consistent source of income; and of course fundraising went on all the time, the ingenuity of members and their friends seemingly unlimited. C. Rowland Johns wrote a number of books, the profits from which went entirely to the League, and the Grateful Dogs' Fund was started to support the clinics, shelters and dogs' homes. (Anyone contributing 5s. or more to the Fund automatically qualified for the 'Jolly Old Dogs Club' – or rather, their dogs did!) Stamps, collected, valued and sold under the guidance of experts like Frank Collie, Margaret Vivian and Louis Cahen, were a small but steady source of profit, all the money going to the clinics.

Nineteen twenty-six was a particularly difficult year for the League, with the opening of two clinics and the Hampton Home

A brand new ambulance, seen here outside the Teddington clinic in 1933.

National Canine Defence Week, 1929: a school lesson in dog care.

putting major pressure on their funds and donations badly hit by the General Strike. But then, in September 1928, came the first National Canine Defence Week, an attempt to publicise the League's work on a nationwide scale.

'Hundreds of cinemas throughout the kingdom have shown our lantern slides,' reported the *Bulletin* that autumn. The League's centres, shelters, clinics and homes threw their doors open to the public, as did many independent breeders; and newspapers gave more space than ever to interviews, features and letters from and about the League and its day-to-day activities. During one interview with C. Rowland Johns, a journalist revealed that he had been advised to have his own dog put down; he was sent to the Hackney clinic, where the dog's sickness was freshly diagnosed and successfully treated; the article which followed was as flattering as it was heartfelt.

'The year 1928 will ever be memorable in the history of the "modern dog" ', wrote Theo Marples, editor of *Our Dogs*, 'for the institution of Canine Defence Week.' The experiment was repeated in 1929, with the new film, *A Dog's Day*, shown in 550 cinemas across the country, as the Week's centrepiece. Although both Weeks had been successful, the planning required each year was too much for an organisation which was still modest in size and working constantly under enormous daily pressure, so they had to be discontinued.

'A few years ago', wrote C. Rowland Johns in the 1922 annual report, 'the average newspaper reader did not concern himself with the adequacy of the punishments for cruelty to dogs – the leniency of the penalty did not interest him. But today every omission of the magistrate . . . is greeted with criticism . . . convictions are now obtained in cases which twenty years ago would not have been taken into court with any chance of success. . . . We do not claim to have done all the good work for animals in the last fifteen or twenty years . . . but we do think we are entitled to be regarded as a force for good and as a force which is always vital and sometimes original.'

The Protection of Animals (Cruelty to Dogs) Act 1933 was certainly original – a Bill piloted through Parliament in record time (thanks to the support of the Home Office) by Sir Robert Gower, the League's Chairman and Treasurer, and an important step forward from the Forfeit Clause of the 1911 Act. Under it, an owner convicted of cruelty to a dog would forfeit his right to keep one *sine die*.

Such a hardening of the law against cruelty was needed, for the League had had to point out on many occasions during the preceding years how rarely the Forfeit Clause was invoked in the courts. Too often convicted owners were allowed to keep their pets, possibly to torture them again. 'If such principles were applied to other crimes we should see the burglar presented with his jemmy on leaving the courtroom,' said the 1923 annual report, adding with some feeling, 'It is regrettable that, when the "bucking mule" has almost disappeared from the music-hall stage, his imitators should be entrusted with the administration of the law.'

The maximum penalty for any act of cruelty to a dog, no matter how appalling, was £25 or three months in jail. Fines of £1 were infinitely more common. The League fought persistently against such leniency and each time a letter of protest from them appeared in the press, penalties did, for a while, become stiffer.

Legislation sometimes had the unintended consequence of provoking further cruelty. The Cattle Disease Order of the early twenties, for example, made many dog-owners afraid to let their dogs out, fearing that they would either be shot or taken away, so many rural dogs were condemned to a life of almost perpetual chaining. The League, trying as ever to be pragmatic, encouraged owners to use the alternative 'wire and post' method, which gave dogs much more freedom of movement, but too many owners cared too little about their dogs, or had no appreciation of how vital exercise was to them.

Chaining remained one of the League's major headaches, hence this new poster. (They had just moved to Victoria Street.)

Even the intervention of the Canine Surgeon to King George V, who, after listing the deleterious effects of chaining, declared that 'if I could not keep a dog except on a chain, I would do without a dog,' had little effect.

The League pursued the cause with all their usual determination, issuing posters and numerous letters to papers up and down the country, and eliciting the help of clergy in pricking the consciences of their dog-owning parishioners, especially in the remoter country districts, where the poor old farm-dog suffered more than most. They also made a film publicising the horrors of prolonged chaining and RSPCA inspectors helped by investigating many cases on the League's behalf.

The indiscriminate shooting of dogs, particularly for trespassing, no matter how brief or harmless the transgression, was another abuse against which the League fought for many years, not least because it infringed in the most elemental way possible the rights of dogs.

A more legitimate anxiety in rural areas was sheep-worrying, but again reaction could be extreme. In Aberdeen in 1925 it was proposed that all strays should be shot on sight if seen between dusk and dawn, while in Durham someone suggested that chauffeurs (*sic*) should receive a capitation grant for killing any loose dogs they saw.

'Boon companions' said the 1932 annual report of this photograph, designed to show that dogs should not be seen as the implacable enemy of sheep.

It was, in fact, illegal to shoot dogs merely because they were trespassing and suspicion of sheep-worrying was hardly an excuse to despatch a possibly quite innocent animal. The laying-down of poison was becoming a prevalent alternative but, gunmen or poisoners, the culprits were just as hard to catch, for they acted fast and just as swiftly buried the evidence. Traps, too, continued to take their small but regular toll of canine lives.

In 1926 the National Farmers Union set out to prove that dogs in the countryside were enough of a pest to justify legislation making it easier to shoot them. While firmly warning dog-owners to take all reasonable care in the countryside, the League could not resist the pointed observation that 'if farmers would train their sheepdogs to beat off marauding dogs, instead of chaining them up for most of their lives, they might suffer less.' Furthermore, they added, 'any farmer found with a shot dog in his field could say that the dog was chasing his stock. A young dog will often run after cows with no intention of harming them, whilst pigs and sheep will stampede

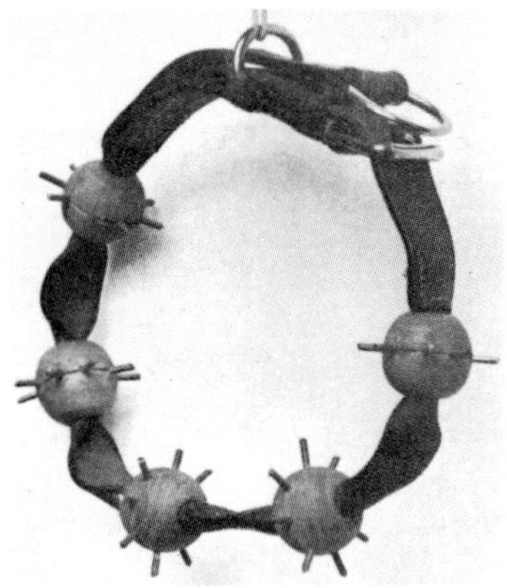

A collar used in training dogs: the kind of cruelty the League were determined to stamp out.

when a dog goes along a footpath, in which case an angry farmer – and farmers are prone to anger – would find his gun a means of venting his general wrath against a particular and possibly innocent dog.'

In 1927 farmers in Northern Ireland succeeded in persuading their government to pass just the kind of legislation the National Farmers Union in Britain were looking for. The League prepared to repel boarders. A correspondent told the *Bulletin* that dog-owners should join the League in much the same way that motorists joined the AA, to have their rights protected.

In the various fields of entertainment, new forms of cruelty replaced those the League had helped to eradicate. 'Perhaps one of the most heartening tributes to our work in opposing cruelty,' C. Rowland Johns told members in 1923, 'is the almost total disappearance of performing dogs . . . from the music-hall stage,' a triumph shared with colleagues in the Performing Animals Defence League. Vigilance, however, was still essential 'in the third-rate theatres in the back streets', in the 'mammoth circuses' at Christmas and at various outdoor shows, where there was a new vogue – the jumping dog, required to leap as high as ten or twelve feet through hoops, some of which, for the added amusement of spectators, were set on fire. By 1936 the League had persuaded the Kennel Clubs of England, Scotland and Ireland to outlaw such excesses at all shows under their control.

The captions say it all . . .

THE CRUEL TRAINER WISHES TO BELIEVE THAT HIS DOGS ENJOY LIFE –

– AS MUCH AS HE DOES!

C. Rowland Johns, with friend, at a meeting in Bristol, 1937. He travelled widely to get the League's message across to dog-owners.

The burgeoning film industry was now giving the League as many headaches as had theatres and music-halls, for film-makers were not covered by the same anti-cruelty laws as theatres: animal trainers in the film business didn't even have to be licenced, and in any case many animals used in films were trained in America, where British law did not apply. The censor in Britain assured the League that he would not pass a film for exhibition if he suspected cruelty to any animal in it, though quite how this was to be established was hard to imagine, most of the cruelty (as with stage acts) going on behind the scenes, during training.

In 1931 the League advised members that 'some good results might be obtained by communicating with Mr Will H. Hays, of Hollywood, who has in hand a task somewhat similar to that of our own film censors. Our representation secured from Mr Hays a sympathetic and characteristically forceful reply, and we were invited to continue to place before him our views on films which come under our notice.'

Not long afterwards the League attended a special conference of the British Board of Film Censors to establish guidelines for the safety and care of animals in films, the outcome of which was the Cinematograph Films (Animals) Act 1937, introduced into the Commons by Sir Robert Gower on behalf of the RSPCA and the League and designed to prevent the showing of any film in which cruelty to animals could be proved.

The newly formed British Broadcasting Corporation also came under fire from the League (and other animal welfare groups), for their 'encouragement of so-called "scientists" who have been permitted to describe revolting experiments which are utterly futile,' as the annual report put it in 1930. 'It seems a thousand pities that this, the greatest potential educational medium the world has ever known, should push the animal welfare movement into the remote background . . .'

In December that year the *Bulletin* compared the intelligence of the BBC with that of the average dog; the BBC came second. The League had been provoked by the Corporation's 'flippant' reaction to a letter from a member who had asked if, in order 'to mitigate the menace to our dogs' nervous systems during the climax of the firework celebrations on 5 November,' the BBC could broadcast 'as noisy a band programme as possible'.

'The BBC ignored the essential seriousness of this request,' thundered the *Bulletin*, 'and referred the matter to the buffoonery department, which proceeded to conjure up an excruciatingly funny (to themselves) word-picture of a dog suffering from a "catherine-wheel complex".' The BBC managed to redeem itself, however, with more positive items about dogs, including the appearance on *In Town Tonight* in 1936 of a number of NCDL dog heroes; and they were unwittingly instrumental in raising valuable funds for the League's Sussex Home in 1939 when a member bought one of those extraordinary new inventions, a television set, and charged her neighbours and friends an entrance fee to watch it.

A minor but still worrying aspect of the 'performing dog' problem were those dogs often to be seen in the streets, aiding beggars and alms-gatherers. They prompted a letter from C. Rowland Johns to *The Times*, pointing out the cruelty of expecting a dog to stand for hours with a hat or other receptacle in his mouth – indeed, of asking it to stand for hours at all without any kind of exercise. No matter how humble their station in life, dogs could rely on the National Canine Defence League to look out for their interests.

Broadcasting House, London, home of the BBC. The League did not care for the Corporation's tone, but it later made amends. *(BBC)*

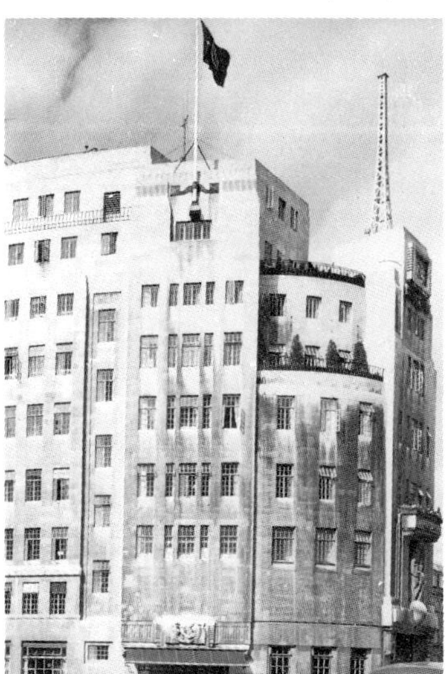

And nor were the League afraid to storm the bastions of their own canine world, in the shape of the major dog shows. In 1938 they launched their campaign against the confinement of dogs for thirty or forty hours at a stretch at the half-dozen or so two-day shows around Britain, of which Cruft's was the most eminent.

The League had first objected in 1934 to the long-established practice of keeping dogs confined, often in cramped, unhygienic conditions, throughout the two days, even where they were needed on only one. Now they were driven to action by the death at Cruft's of a bull-terrier who had torn away the wire and wood of his cage, tried to escape and been hanged by his own chain.

The campaign created 'the greatest controversy in the pedigree-dog world for a long time', reported the *Bulletin* with relish. 'The heat engendered has been super-tropical.' 'The KC does not need

Cruft's, *c.* 1939.

to be taught its duty to the canine race . . . by the National Canine Defence League,' railed the Kennel Club, who ridiculed the claim that dogs suffered in any way at these shows, ignoring the evidence supplied in shoals of letters from breeders and other exhibitors.

At last someone decided to take the League's objections seriously. The 1939 Blackpool show was reorganised to take account of their suggestion that no dog should be kept overnight: the League called it 'sectionalising'. The result? A record entry of 3,200, a third up on the previous year. 'A gratifying feature was the wholehearted co-operation of Blackpool Corporation,' wrote C. Rowland Johns. 'They [gave] a magnificent 100-guinea cup for the best dog in the show; and to crown their generosity they provided the show with its Chairman in the distinguished person of the Mayor, Alderman W. Rostron Duckworth MP.'

The callous destruction of so many dogs; draconian quarantine regulations; dog-fighting and badger-baiting (cruel to both badger and dog); the use of draught dogs (now restricted to certain European countries, such as Belgium, but in due course outlawed even there, partly through the League's efforts); the unthinking use of chemicals and poisons where dogs could get at them; the doping of greyhounds; tail-cropping and rounding the ears of hounds; feeding dogs inadequately and ignoring signs of pain or ill-health (the *Bulletin* ran regular features on diet and health care) – these were

Lassie, rescued by the League in Brighton after being thrown from an upstairs window by her owner.

just a few of the many other forms of cruelty to dogs that men devised and which the League spent much of their time trying to subvert through education and, if all else failed, legislation.

Sometimes the League's enthusiasm for defending dogs' rights could take them down bizarre paths. Such was surely the case with their campaign against bye-laws first introduced in Kensington, in London, in 1922, making it an offence to allow dogs to foul the footway. The League were outraged, the more so when some councils appointed a 'Nuisance Inspector' to examine the behaviour of passing dogs, with the result that many an owner found himself paying a fine for his pet's inability to read and comprehend the new regulations.

'Perhaps London University will establish a Diploma Course for ambitious young men with keen eyesight,' sarcastically suggested the *Bulletin*. 'Training for such an illustrious profession can hardly be left to the correspondence schools.'

The League's objection to these bye-laws (the spirit of which they understood – they gave out advice on training dogs in these matters as with everything else) was that to force dogs into the gutter, as the councils insisted, was to court disaster from passing cars and lorries; they cited several instances in which dogs had been injured (and in one case killed) in just such circumstances. It would also, they claimed, discourage dog-ownership in towns, despite the fact that they were, in the view of the police, the best protection against burglaries.

It is difficult to feel much sympathy for the League's views (it couldn't have been *that* hard in the 1920s to pick a time when nothing was coming), particularly if you have ever fallen foul, so to speak, of a dog's willingness to, as the *Bulletin* delicately put it, 'follow the dictates of nature on the pavement'. Yet to the League these new measures, adopted by an increasing number of boroughs through the twenties and thirties, provided further proof that, as the *Bulletin* insisted in 1937, a 'constant erosion of the rights of dogs is in progress'.

On the other hand, running over dogs *had* become a minority sport among motorists, who sometimes wrote to car magazines boasting about their prowess. One claimed to have killed eighteen in two years; another – 'out-Heroding Herod', as the *Bulletin* put it – claimed twenty in twelve months. And as if to prove the League's point about dogs' rights, in 1925 a county court judge, speaking in a case brought by an owner against a motorist who had run over his dog, said that he could not find that a dog had any rights on the roads whatsoever.

In answer, the League insisted that a dog 'has the right of "passing and re-passing", he has a right to cross the road, he has a right to walk along it'. If damages for injury are to be claimed, however, he must be shown to have been under his owner's control at the time. But 'one of the greatest fallacies is to believe that "under control" means that a dog must be on a lead. A dog following to heel or walking at the side of his owner is legally under control and a motorist who runs such a dog down is liable to pay damages . . .'

Around this time there was considerable debate about the necessity for leads, and about whether they, too, infringed on dogs' rights. But as traffic increased, notably when the cheap family car was introduced in the late thirties, discussions of a philosophical nature about such methods of restraint became irrelevant: dogs not under control caused accidents (in which they were usually the greatest sufferers) and their right to use the highway with impunity, sharing it equally with the motor-car, as the League had advocated in the

One driver who seems unlikely ever to want to run over a dog: from a League campaign against callous motorists, 1937.

early years of the century, had to give way to the *force majeure* of the internal combustion engine, as the League itself acknowledged when it answered the question, 'How can I prevent my dog being run over by motors?' as early as 1924:

> The golden way is, of course, to train a dog to keep to heel, but it is not every dog who will forego the delight of darting across the road to interview a fellow 'four-legger' . . . although in law a dog . . . has the right to use the roadway for a legitimate purpose, a reliance upon abstract theory is unsatisfactory when your dog has been badly maimed or killed . . . In a busy town the early morning is the best time for exercising dogs, for the heavy traffic comes up later than the mushrooms . . .

In 1930 the League persuaded the AA to equip some of its 'road scouts' (many of whom were trained in first aid) with 'humane

An AA 'road scout' in the 1930s. They were trained to help injured dogs. *(Automobile Association)*

pistols', so that if they came across an injured dog and could do nothing to save him, he could be put out of his misery quickly and painlessly; and the new Road Traffic Act, though making no special provisions for dogs, other than to oblige motorists to stop if they ran over one, did help them obliquely by forcing all motorists to take out insurance against 'third-party' risk. The main effect of this measure, the League assured dog-owners, would be to eliminate the road-hog, who would henceforth avoid accidents for fear of becoming an unacceptable risk to insurers – a somewhat over-optimistic forecast.

In 1937 the League printed two-and-a-half million copies of a leaflet on road safety, aimed at dog-owners and motorists alike, which they distributed nationwide in a major (and expensive) effort to heighten public awareness of the need for care, consideration and common sense on all sides.

Another sort of scout and another type of heroics: John Earl, who rescued the dog in the picture from under the wheels of an express in 1923 and received the League's medal.

It cost 3s. 6d. to send a dog 100 miles by rail in 1922 and it was a service much used. The League worked tirelessly to ensure the comfort and safety of dogs in transit. We have seen that they had a lively relationship with the railway companies, but it was by no means all bad; the companies often cooperated quite happily with them (they probably knew better than to do otherwise).

In 1922, for instance, they allowed the League, free of charge, to put up thousands of posters at stations throughout Britain, stressing the importance of 'packing' dogs properly, even providing the necessary labour; some continued to overlook their own bye-laws in allowing dogs to travel in passenger compartments with their owners; and they provided drinking-bowls and comfortable 'kennels' when a dog had to travel in the guard's van. No dog needed to contemplate a train journey in Britain between the wars with apprehension, thanks to the National Canine Defence League's unremitting vigilance.

In the case of buses and trams, vigilance was required to make sure that dogs could travel on them at all: they were banned here, permitted there, and the League fought hard to get a common policy established (namely, no bans!), citing the example of the capital, where for years dogs had been allowed to travel on the top deck without inconvenience to other passengers.

Municipal landlords provided the chance to mount a few effective campaigns of resistance, too. 'Get rid of your dog – or get out!' was the edict of, among others, Huddersfield council, in Yorkshire, in 1936. Backed by the League, the 100 tenants concerned organised a petition and protest meetings and eventually persuaded the council to back down. 'The tenants held a celebration dinner afterwards,' reported the *Bulletin*, 'at which one dog-owner exclaimed, "Thank God for such societies as the National Canine Defence League." '

'It is not to be denied,' C. Rowland Johns had written ten years earlier about another case, 'that if dogs are not properly looked after in congested areas they will cause a certain amount of annoyance, but . . . it is somewhat of a stretch of the imagination to hold that they are necessarily a menace to the public health' – the reason invariably given for getting rid of dogs from tenements or flats.

More happily, the League were involved from the outset of such schemes in providing dogs for the blind. In 1933, for example, they supplied the recently formed 'Guide Dogs for the Blind' with six Alsatians for training, and a number of C. Rowland Johns's books were translated into braille.

A Liverpool blind man and his guide dog, 1933.

In 1933 the League inaugurated its Argus Medal, designed by sculptor Frank Bowcher and awarded in recognition of long and distinguished service to dogs. The first recipients were Miss M. F. Clifton, a member of the League Council, Mrs W. Bently Capper, secretary of the Manchester centre, and (posthumously) publisher and animal-welfare activist, Ernest Bell. The Medal was not easily won – only six were awarded between its inception and its replacement in 1978 by the Phyllis Meyer Argus Award, which to date has also had six winners. And of course silver and bronze medals continued to be awarded to numerous human and canine heroes, the men, women and children involved proving yet again that for every perpetrator of cruelty to dogs there was someone prepared to be utterly selfless on their behalf, and the dog heroes demonstrating the intelligence and devotion which in the view of so many dog-lovers set them apart from other animals and earned them the right to a special place in human affections.

* * *

As those now well-documented storm clouds gathered over Europe in the late 1930s, the League, confident that no one this time would infer that there would be very little for them to do, set about preparing their members for the gloomy days ahead – and preparing themselves, too. This time the war, they knew, would come to the cities of Britain in a far bigger way than a few bombs thrown from Zeppelins: the devastation wrought in Spain had made that clear. Would they continue to have a headquarters from which to direct operations? Time to worry about that when it happened. In the meantime, consider the dogs.

'If a great, overwhelming onslaught were made on us,' said the *Bulletin* in February 1939, 'we should endeavour to save our own pets, but the suffering of animals would be unimaginable . . . The Government is asking for a million ARP workers for human beings; they appear to have no plans for animal protection.'

Bleak as the prospects were, there was always hope. As the League said after Munich: 'When the war clouds were at their blackest, one bright ray illumined the gloom, and that was the realisation that British dog-lovers were more concerned for their canine friends' safety than for their own. All through the weeks of throbbing tension that preceded the Munich conference, the League's telephones had scarcely an idle moment. "Where can I get a gas-mask for my dog?" . . . "What do you advise me to do with my dog in the event of air-raids?" . . . "Where can I find accommodation for my dog in the country?" Our clinic superintendents, too, were bombarded for days with similar queries . . . Fortunately, we had the foresight to prepare in good time for such an emergency.'

Indeed they had. Early in 1937 they had experimented with gas-masks for dogs, and they suggested to members that they construct 'gas-proof chambers' for themselves and their pets ('two ordinary-sized dogs or one large dog consume as much air as a human being'); in 1939 they were to introduce a 'gas-proof kennel', 'the chief drawback [of which] seems to be the initial cost of £3 3s. 0d. upwards,' said the *Bulletin*, adding, 'but presumably if there were a considerable demand the price could be reduced,' a faith in the altruism of businessmen which can only be called endearing.

They also arranged with dog-loving car-owners to ferry dogs to the country in the event of an emergency and, through the press and the BBC, obtained promises of sanctuary from a long list of country-dwellers.

'The League has thus accomplished much spadework in preparation for any future crisis,' said the *Bulletin* in the autumn of 1938. The Munich panic had subsided, but no one was under any illusion about the hardships that lay ahead.

The greatness of a nation and its moral progress can be judged by the way its animals are treated.

Mahatma Ghandi

4 'Heroic and unflinching'

Survival – and disaster, 1939–1953

'It is not going to be an easy task to write the Report of the League's history in 1939,' C. Rowland Johns told members a few months after Prime Minister Chamberlain had finally conceded that Adolf Hitler was not a decent type after all. 'With a great part of the world at war, our work might seem to be dwarfed by comparison with the great events, and yet we feel that, while the British Empire and France are fighting against inhumanity and cruelty in their extremest manifestations, your League's work is in harmonic sequence with that struggle. In a lesser sphere and in a smaller degree the League has done what it could to soften the impact of war and to minimise suffering to dogs and dog-owners.'

The clinics were certainly doing what they could: they helped a record 82,000 animals during 1939, a figure swelled by 'the September crisis', when advice and encouraging words saved thousands of animals from destruction as owners took an understandably despondent look at the future and decided that there would be no place for their pets in a country where at best they would be hard put to it to feed them and at worst they might find themselves overrun by Nazis, who were not thought to be animal-lovers.

The newly invented 'gas-proof chamber'.

'Wait and see,' advised the ever-hopeful League. It was a sad fact that many of those who brought their pets to the clinics and insisted on having them put down later regretted their decision and came back hoping to find replacements. One trend the League was glad to note was the reluctance of hard-pressed owners to turn their dogs adrift; if they had problems, they went to the clinics.

The League produced a number of leaflets offering advice on how to cope with the anticipated emergencies and shortages of war, including what to do if Britain was invaded ('Dogs and the Invader', leaflet no. 489). Guard-dogs should be kept indoors 'to give timely warning of the approach of paratroops . . . kept outside on a chain, [they] will be easy victims to enemy tommy-guns.' Large-scale hoarding of dog-food was not advised, though 'a bottle of water for the dog will be useful'. As dogs could not be officially evacuated, owners were warned to make plans for moving them early.

As for gas attacks, tear gas did not affect dogs, the leaflet pointed out, but others – mustard gas and lewisite – certainly did and owners were reminded about the home-made gas-proof boxes which the League had devised: simple wooden cartons large enough for the dog to stand up in and made gas-tight 'by pasting up all chinks with stout paper'. The hole in the lid through which the dog was admitted would be covered with wire mesh and, during an attack, with 'a piece of flannel saturated in a fairly strong solution of some chlorine disinfectant'. Gloss-painting the whole box would help to absorb some of the gas.

December 1940: an injured victim of a German air-raid will not be parted from his dog.

Another leaflet ('Poison Gas and Domestic Pets', no. 491) gave detailed instructions on applying first-aid to canine victims of gas. It was essential to carry with you at all times two dusters, a piece of soap and a cocoa tin containing bleach powder (chloride of lime); using them required several buckets of water and, since the process was not exactly the work of a moment, more time than was likely to be at an owner's disposal in an emergency, but apparently the treatment worked.

Leaflet no. 486 gave advice on air-raid precautions for dogs and cats, including the suggestion that nervous dogs should be given a five-grain aspirin tablet to calm them down at the first sound of an attack.

Feeding dogs was to be one of the major problems of this war, as it had been of the earlier one. By Christmas 1939 27,000 owners had written asking for the League's leaflet, 'War-time Dog Food'. The League advised owners to start local meat-buying clubs and it wasn't long before they were able to supply lists of firms willing to supply meat parcels for dogs. (As usual with the League, the lists, if not the parcels, cost no more than the price of a stamp.) The meat was most likely to be horseflesh, for once rationing had begun the human population soon turned to meat that before the war had been

A sandbagged reception-point for urgently-needed aluminium, with British bulldogs on hand to encourage donations. *(Imperial War Museum)*

generally regarded as suitable only for animals – offal, for example – but the *Bulletin* was pleased to report that 'sheeps' heads, including practically all the bone, can be made edible by high-pressure cooking'.

A breadless diet for dogs was particularly recommended, for the League knew that cereal-based foodstuffs such as biscuits would become increasingly difficult to obtain as the war dragged on. Some owners gave their pets stale bread to eat, only to find that this was an offence under the Milled Wheaten Substances (Restrictions) Order of 1940. The increase in domestic poultry and rabbits meant that there were far fewer scraps left over for dogs and by 1943 the League were calling the situation worse than in 1917–18.

Vets agreed that potatoes, long a taboo food for dogs, would not do them any harm provided they took plenty of exercise; but when the League approached Lord Woolton, the Minister for Food, about the possibility of lifting the ban on giving them to dogs, the Minister refused, saying he wanted to encourage humans, not dogs, to eat more potatoes and less bread. In one London borough kitchen and abattoir waste was sterilised, minced and concentrated to produce up to a thousand 2lb. jars a week of food fit for poultry, pigs and dogs, at a shilling a jar.

At least the League, together with the RSPCA, managed to get guide dogs a special food concession, though after first raising the

'Salvage!' was the *Bulletin*'s caption to this picture in its Summer 1941 issue. A tribute to the efforts being made to convert kitchen waste into food for dogs and other animals.

'On your way!' Dogs were again proving their worth to the army as messengers.

issue in October 1939 it took them two years to get the Government to act.

The League suggested that one way in which dogs could help their masters to conserve food – and in doing so perhaps improve their own image, for some of the same hostility to dogs that the League had had to struggle against during the First World War was quick to surface during this conflict, too – was by catching rats. 'It is conservatively estimated', the League reported early in the war, 'that rats consume or destroy £75,000,000-worth of foodstuffs in this country every year – sufficient to maintain the entire population of the British Isles for two weeks.' By 1941 they could justly claim that the guard-dogs of Britain, through their work at airfields, factories and other storage centres, 'have saved many precious shiploads of food from destruction by vermin' – food they themselves were forbidden to share, the *Bulletin* pointed out. The League even ran nationwide competitions offering prizes to the best rat-catchers.

People had no right to feel hostile towards dogs, for in other ways, too, they served the nation in its hour of need. In 1941 the League, with the RSPCA, was asked to establish a large pool of dogs for war work. Airedales, Alsatians, Bull-terriers, Collies and Lurchers were the chosen breeds: large dogs all. At first it wasn't easy to find enough for all the duties the armed forces had in mind for their canine recruits, many larger dogs having been the first to go in that early bout of fear-driven destruction; but eventually the numbers were made up, for owners of those that remained had great difficulty feeding them adequately and were only too willing to let the Government take care of them for the duration (at the end of which they would be returned with full honours and a citation).

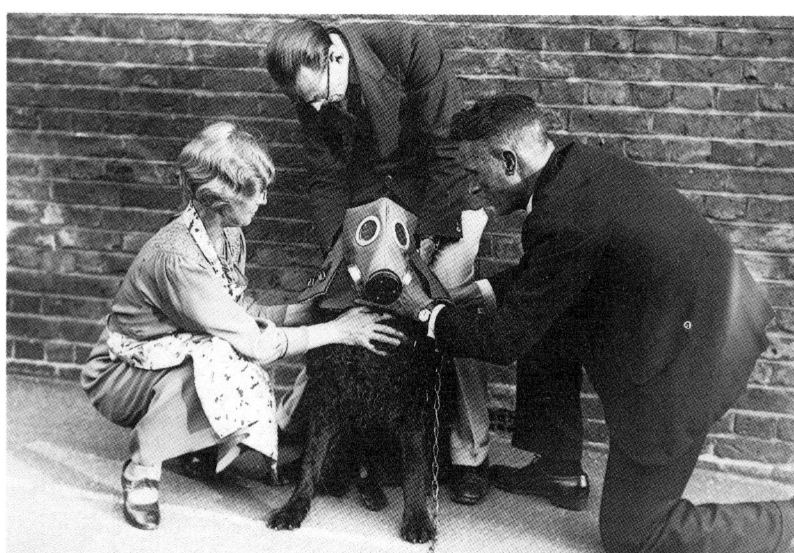

Enough to frighten us, let alone the Germans: a canine guinea-pig tries out a new type of gas-mask. *(L. F. Poole)*

Keeping the Forces warm with dog-wool, 1944.

A further canine contribution to the war effort was through the combings of the longhaired breeds; this 'dog-wool' was used to knit clothing for the troops (as it had been on a smaller scale in the earlier war). The spinning was done by hand on old-fashioned spinning wheels – some of it, through the influence of the London School of Weaving, in Highland crofts – at a cost of 8d. an ounce. Seaboot stockings and mittens were the favourite end-products. The scheme was abandoned in 1941 because of difficulties both in finding spinners and in getting the wool to them, but the League continued to organise collections of combings from members throughout the war, passing them on to volunteer groups to deal with: the summer 1945 issue of the *Bulletin* shows a striking seaman's jumper knitted entirely from dog-wool and worn by a merchant seaman from a ship 'adopted' by a group of WVS volunteers.

Although the greatest blow to befall the League during the war was probably the necessity to move offices in 1945 from Victoria Street, where the lease had run out, to Clifford Street, in the West End – there was some compensation in the magnificence of the new surroundings, notably a beautiful staircase with paintings by James Thornhill – they were regular victims of German bombing raids on the capital. All their properties in and around London were damaged at one time or another. 'We suffered even more in 1944 from flying-bombs and rocket-bombs than we had done in the various attacks which were known as "blitzes",' reported C. Rowland Johns (whose son, Pilot Officer Rowland Johns, was now the League's Assistant Secretary). Typical of the response to the bombardment was that of the Hackney clinic on the day it received a direct hit. The vet arrived 'to find it a mere shell, with the roof, windows and most of the flooring missing and nearly all the equipment destroyed'. Undeterred, he set up a rickety table on the pavement outside and proceeded to business as usual.

The Clifford Street offices themselves, having survived the war with relatively minor damage, were gutted by fire in December 1945, just as renovation work was being completed; the staff were left without heat or water at the busiest, and coldest, time of the year; the temptation to stay at home must have been overwhelming, but no one gave in to it.

Around that time C. Rowland Johns wrote a piece, 'A Thousand Nights of Bombing', for the *American Humane Review* in which he gave a vivid account of those nights 'when whole cities flamed red to the sky and thousands of explosions shocked the mind and soul', and then, when that was over, men and animals alike had to endure 'the menacing, air-grinding V1 that seems to roar: "I'm coming straight for you",' and the V2, 'which drops from the stratosphere

Thorn, a specially trained German Shepherd, leads the hunt for survivors of a V1 raid on a hospital, 1945. *(Imperial War Museum)*

without warning and makes a crater big enough to hold five or six Fifth-Avenue omnibuses'. It was broken glass that injured most animals, filling their eyes with fine powder or simply cutting them to pieces.

In February 1944 a 2,000lb. bomb fell in the gardens of the Hampton Dogs' Home and Hospital; miraculously, no staff or dogs were injured, but it left a crater which required 900 tons of rubble to level it. At the Camberwell clinic on one wartime morning there were eighty-five owners with their patients waiting to be seen by a single vet: his colleagues were dealing with emergencies elsewhere.

There was a shortage of staff, anyway: before the end of the war, all men below the age of forty-five had been called up. Fortunately, no one from the League was more than a minor casualty of the war and all returned to active duty of a different and much more welcome kind with the League as soon as hostilities were over.

Dogs were forbidden entry to air-raid shelters in 1940, a shortsighted policy which often meant that wardens had trouble getting people to go down them if it meant leaving their pets behind. In Kensington, London, the chief air-raid warden, Sir Charles Souter, provided space and labour for the League and the RSPCA jointly to build a shelter especially for dogs in Kensington Gardens. (The satisfaction of this achievement, and of maintaining their work generally, was just about the only way the League found to celebrate its golden jubilee in 1941, which otherwise, of necessity, went unmarked.)

The reaction of dogs to the air-raids was far less hysterical and

Ambulancemen and stretcher parties wait for another 'call-out' after an air-raid in March 1940, the station dog at their side as always. *(Imperial War Museum)*

The dog-shelter in Kensington Gardens, London, 1940.

dangerous than the authorities had anticipated. The Government had set up a special committee to deal with the expected problem (doubtless by shooting anything that moved on four legs) but in the event the animals often behaved with more composure than their human masters. Nor were they immune to grief. One poor dog typified the reaction of many. Just before Christmas 1940, an entire household was killed by a direct hit on their home; only their dog survived. He was inconsolable and would not be moved from the rubble, sitting on top of it for five days and refusing all aid, except for a little water. A vet from a nearby League clinic went to the site to see if he could help, but there was nothing to be done except to put the half-starved and near-demented animal out of his misery 'and to write his epitaph in the old, familiar way – "faithful unto death" '.

Any hope of legislation in favour of dogs had to be abandoned, of course, while the war was on, no private members' Bills being allowed time in the Commons; but the League were disappointed to find that, even after the war, nothing could be advanced, so full was the new Labour government's legislative programme.

The League's own programme of help (and self-help), however, went on regardless, affected by the war, naturally, but never entirely brought to a standstill.

The Licence Fund continued to be a source of help to poor owners and increasingly the taxman showed the warmer side of his nature, as the League discovered in 1939, when on one day they received sixty-three applications for licences, all of them sent in by the district tax inspector. The police were also very cooperative. Such goodheartedness had a beneficial side-effect: coming from such sources, these applications did not have to be checked, enabling the League to issue the new licences without delay.

Of course, life wouldn't be the delight it so often is if such institutional common sense wasn't balanced by equally impressive examples of official crassness. We need proceed no further than the autumn of 1940 to find just such an example. It was then, amid the turmoil of war and the threat of imminent invasion, that the police in Ealing were moved to bring a case against a man who had been looking after a friend's dog while he went away for a week. The dog disappeared, the police found it, the guardian expressed his gratitude and then the police said, 'I say, I say, I say, do you have a licence to keep this animal?' 'Well, I'm just looking after it, but the owner certainly has.' 'But you do not?' 'No, officer.' 'In that case, you had better accompany me to the station.' And thus it was that a bemused samaritan found himself in Ealing court, probably wishing that he'd been called up after all.

The League, hearing of the case, realised at once its wider implications: if the samaritan was found guilty it would set an

Pets from bombed-out homes are cared for by a team of volunteers 'somewhere in the south of England', as the *Bulletin* was obliged to put it.

awkward precedent for all other owners who, caring about the welfare of their dogs, arranged for someone else to look after them temporarily. The League provided the defendant with all the help necessary to convince the court that one and all were having their time wasted and the case was swiftly thrown out.

In 1939 the League paid for 2,385 licences – 'just imagine the happiness in all those homes when our help arrived!', as the *Bulletin* joyously exclaimed – and in 1940 another 2,000-odd owners were helped, including the lonely mother of a sailor lost in the *Royal Oak*, whose dog she saw as her only link with her dead son.

After the war the League once again tried to get the tax reformed by lowering the age at which it first became due for a puppy from six months to eight weeks but, although they had the support of, among others, the National Farmers Union, nothing came of their efforts.

Throughout the war and the years that followed, the League never gave up on its main aim of preventing cruelty in all its forms.

The fight against vivisection, for so long the linchpin of the League's campaigns against the maltreatment of dogs, had of necessity to be postponed during the war, although it is clear that even by then the League, though continuing to abhor and oppose the practice, saw it as less of a problem than it had been and one which, for all their own and other people's efforts, seemed highly unlikely ever to be totally eradicated. On the other hand, there *had* been some

Business as usual – the Hackney clinic the morning after a German raid, 1944.

'What's the queue like?' One of the clinics, *c.* 1945. They were invariably full.

helpful legislation, much of it instigated by the League. They had done all that seemed possible.

Not that they intended to give up the fight altogether. The December 1946 issue of the *Bulletin* carried an extract from an article in the *New York Journal American* by Dr J. Howard Crum, a well-known veterinarian, making it clear that, as far as he was concerned, no good had been accomplished by vivisection of dogs that could not have been secured by less cruel methods. 'I could not, and do not, say that certain results have not been obtained from vivisection – but they have been obtained at a terrible price in agony and unspeakable anguish, and moreover could have been obtained otherwise . . . The vast majority of operations upon dogs are useless, senseless and unnecessary.'

Chaining, particularly in rural areas, was a problem that refused to go away. In 1939 dog-lovers in East Anglia got together and devised an unusual scheme to combat it. They announced that they were anxious to take dogs out for daily walks, but, alas, they had no dogs of their own. The infirm and others genuinely unable to exercise their pets took full advantage of this offer, but there was a second major target: farmers (and others) who kept their dogs chained up for long periods.

Here the approach was a subtle one. It was implied not so much that the exercise would benefit the dog – owners who were so indifferent to their animals' needs were unlikely to be moved by considerations of that kind – as that the farmer would be doing the deprived dog-lover a great service in giving him the chance to enjoy the company of a canine friend. It was with a feeling of great beneficence, therefore, that such owners graciously yielded to the group's pleas for help; and, as the *Bulletin* recognised, 'once the concession is granted, not only will the dog have freedom for a spell each day, but also there will be opportunity for a tactful suggestion at well-chosen moments that the rigour of the chaining might be still further relaxed.'

Once the war had begun, chaining became even more prevalent, as owners found themselves preoccupied by other duties for long periods, or so many of them claimed. 'This new excuse for chaining has to some extent offset the beneficial effect of the League's persistent campaign against this evil,' said the annual report for 1941. Posters and leaflets were once again widely distributed (the League having had the foresight to print large stocks before the war).

The League worried that, with the return of traffic to the roads after the war, chaining would once again be resorted to by lazy owners as an alternative to letting dogs roam the streets (or, heaven forbid, taking them out for a walk). Many council tenants said that it was stipulated in their rent books that dogs had to be kept chained. The League had for a long time been proposing a third alternative –

From the *Bulletin*, *c.* 1946.

training dogs in road safety, a theme they were to take up strongly in the postwar years, working with the RSPCA and the Royal Society for the Prevention of Accidents to run dog road-safety schemes all over the country.

Greyhounds – who were allowed to race throughout the war – were another special case of neglect and maltreatment on whom the League kept a close but, by their own admission, largely impotent eye: only the police had any jurisdiction over the running of tracks, including the many unlicensed ones where facilities for the dogs were poor and no veterinary care was ever given. The League did manage to expose the scandal of doping and, in 1949, to start a 'home-finding' service for retired greyhounds (who, once they had stopped winning, 'were', as the *Bulletin* euphemistically put it, 'not esteemed'), an idea which was so successful that the following year they placed over six hundred of these amiable pets with new and altogether more caring owners.

Racing greyhounds at Wembley Stadium. After the war the League started a homefinding service for 'retired' greyhounds. *(GRA)*

One previously controversial subject about which the League clearly had a change of mind was the law regarding quarantine. By 1950 they were actually supporting the six-month period against which they had previously so often protested, on the perfectly understandable grounds that '[it] has eliminated hydrophobia scares and their associated muzzling orders for the last thirty years'.

Rather than try to change a system that was working effectively, they preferred to help those for whom the cost was prohibitive and threatened to force them to abandon beloved pets. One of their great successes was the Quarantine Fund for Refugee Dogs, launched in 1939. The refugees in question came over from Europe in their hundreds in the company of owners who often had nothing but the clothes they stood up in and yet frequently sacrificed their own needs for the safety of their dogs.

Typical was the case of Marko, a three-year-old St Bernard, whose mistress, a penniless refugee from Vienna, had brought him up from his bottle-feeding puppy days and would not be parted from him even during flight from the invading Germans. In a letter to the League, she described meeting up with Marko again after months of enforced absence: 'Hardly had I entered the quarantine kennels than I heard the barking of my dog. Out of thousands I should have recognised it again. It sounded so sad . . . But then, when he saw me really and truly before him, I realised how an animal could show his pleasure at meeting a human being . . . I shall always be indebted to you.'

Less typical but no less sincere was the actress Mrs Patrick

Teaching schoolchildren about road safety for dogs became a priority for the League after the war. This picture was taken in 1948.

Campbell, who became a voluntary exile from England rather than go through the pain of being parted from her pet Pekingese, Moonbeam, for the second time. In 1935 she had brought him back from America and been forced to watch him being taken away for the statutory six months.

'When I arrived at the quarantine kennels,' she said, 'and saw the nervous agony, the utter misery and bewilderment on his little face, and that my voice and my petting had no power to stop his sobs and trembling, I telephoned to the Ministry of Agriculture to send a conveyance at once so that I could cross that evening to Boulogne . . . a few days later I sailed back to New York. It was easier for me to sacrifice the happiness of giving my talent to my English audience and to lose a salary of £100 per week than to break my little dog's heart.' Four years later 'Mrs Campbell is still of the same mind,' reported the *Bulletin*, 'but she and the little dog are now living in Paris "to be nearer England".'

In 1940 the League's funds helped many soldiers to pay quarantine bills for dogs they had befriended in France and Belgium and somehow managed to bring home with them, a number of them becoming regimental mascots. But if the League anticipated an even bigger problem when the war ended, they were in for an agreeable surprise from, of all sources, the Government, who in 1945 introduced a cheap-rate scheme for the transport and quarantine of servicemen's dogs being brought back from any of the various theatres of war, no matter how remote.

Charges were on a sliding scale according to rank: up to corporal, for instance, you paid £5; an officer was asked for £20. According to the League, who helped to publicise the scheme, over a thousand dogs had been returned to their owners' hearthsides by the end of 1946 who might otherwise have been abandoned overseas.

In the immediate postwar years, the League also resumed their campaigns against dog-fighting, badger-baiting, the maltreatment of performing dogs (notably in film-making), illegal shooting, unscrupulous dog-dealers and breeders, and dog-stealing; and of course the railway and bus companies were not allowed to forget their obligations to their canine passengers.

The League took quiet satisfaction from the knowledge that the reform in two-day dog shows for which they had campaigned before the war had by the late forties been almost universally accepted.

As for the poor old stray, he was never far from the League's thoughts. Although conditions for the caring of strays understandably deteriorated during the war, particularly in police kennels, the League felt that by 1948 they were entitled to remind Chuter Ede, the Home Secretary, of the agreement reached before the war with one of his predecessors that dogs in police custody would be properly and humanely housed. Mr Ede duly promised that government inspectors would, as under the previous agreement, ensure that police stations were doing everything necessary to guarantee the reasonable comfort of dogs in their care. With the war out of the way, the League were able to turn their attention more fully to the perpetual problem of strays, looking to extend their facilities for housing them and finding them new homes.

(Below and opposite, top) Dogs were by no means the only pets the League helped or gave owners advice about . . .

Despite the war, and the fact that by the end of it they had 'lost all trace' of almost 2,000 members and donors (membership in 1946 was down to 1,200, lower than at any time since the earliest years of the century), the League's income had continued, through good husbandry, to keep pace with the demands made on their various funds, though not without difficulty. In 1940 they had earned or were donated £9,000, including £550 from the sale of luminous collars and leads, foreign stamps, silver paper, drinking troughs, literature, calendars and the *Bulletin*. Legacies almost doubled the

National Canine Defence League — Leaflet No. 474

THE TORTOISE

Its Care and Feeding

Many Tortoises are brought to the National Canine Defence League's Clinics for treatment, and their ailments are frequently due to a lack of understanding of their needs.

WHERE TORTOISES COME FROM.

The species of Tortoise commonly sold in street markets and elsewhere is the Greek Tortoise, and is found in countries bordering on the Mediterranean Sea. It is, therefore, a sub-tropical creature, and although its hold on life in colder latitudes is remarkably tenacious, it stands a far greater chance of a long and happy life if its comfort is given due consideration.

BUYING A TORTOISE.

When buying a Tortoise, select one that is clear of eye, has an unbroken shell, and is lively and bright in appearance, retracting its head and legs quickly when picked up. Reject any with broken shells (a crack that has healed or been obviously repaired is not a drawback); with saliva dripping from the mouth (indicative of pneumonia); or with limbs and head lolling weakly from the shell.

figure. The running of the League's homes, shelters and clinics, however, cost nearly £6,500 and rent on the Victoria Street offices was £633.

By 1945 income had gone up considerably, while expenditure had actually been brought down: this was largely because of the enforced cutback in the production of printed material, while office salaries were lower simply because most of the staff were away fighting. The Licence Fund was in surplus to the tune of £10,000.

After the war things improved, despite the general hardship. In 1948, the League were able for the first time to report an annual income of over £50,000 – but, as they warned members, this was due less to the eightfold increase in membership, as beleaguered owners turned naturally to the society whose concern for the welfare of dogs was most widely known, than to 'an unusually large amount received in legacies', a phenomenon which could not be relied upon to repeat itself. Indeed, 1948 saw a 'severe deficit' in the income-and-expenditure account, largely because of expansion and repair work on homes and clinics, together with a big increase in the production of literature of all kinds as the League got back into its educating and campaigning stride (and the cost of paper rose steeply).

By 1950, expenditure had exceeded income by over £6,000 for the third year running and the League were forced to draw on capital to maintain their services. Nevertheless, they still managed to introduce a free public liability (third-party) insurance policy for full members, covering all claims against dogs up to £1,000.

By 1952, membership had levelled out at 12,000 (the minimum annual subscription was still only two guineas) and everything seemed set fair for an expansive and successful future.

Bombed-out evacuees in Plymouth, 1941. Life was often primitive for evacuees, but considerate owners always found room for the family dog, as here. *(Imperial War Museum)*

You may have noticed that the *Bulletin* is mentioned as regularly in this chapter as in the last, even though the League had so dramatically to reduce their output of literature. This is because they had promised members to keep publishing it, no matter how difficult the problems became.

'Small and unassuming in appearance,' as the 1939 annual report called it, the *Bulletin* was nevertheless a widely popular source of news, advice and firmly-voiced opinion, so much so that in the middle of the war the League actually received complaints that it wasn't appearing regularly enough! Doubts about its future did arise in 1943, but somehow the League – 'short of staff, paper and time,' as they told impatient subscribers – kept their promise.

'One of the notable phenomena of our . . . history', wrote C. Rowland Johns in the 1945 annual report, 'is the survival of all our activities . . . during the long war just ended,' though he did admit to having had occasionally to make what he called 'variations and adjustments' to routine.

The League had indeed fought a good war. As one newspaper said after reading the 1944 annual report, 'This booklet presents a record of truly magnificent service heroically and unflinchingly rendered under extreme peril . . .' Once again the League had had to fight for the right of the dog to be fed, to be sheltered – and indeed, as in the First World War, to be allowed to live at all in the face of human deprivation and the resultant hardening of attitudes to dogs.

The dog-owners of Britain – including many of those languishing in prisoner-of-war camps in Europe and the Far East, as well as those still on active service, none of whose feelings, as usual, were taken into account by those who hated dogs – had good cause to be grateful for the League's efforts to ensure the continuing place of dogs in the community. Sir Robert Gower, speaking at the April 1946 annual meeting of the League – the first for seven years – told members that they could 'take no small pride in the fact that conditions for dogs have been so well maintained', a characteristic piece of understatement.

Anxious owners await the judge's verdict at Cruft's, 1950.

The end of the war did not bring instant joy and light to the world of dogs. Food rationing for them as well as for humans was to persist until 1952 and the immediate postwar years were ones of austerity and continued belt-tightening as this country, like so many others, struggled to recover from six years of global conflict.

One victim of rationing for whom the League was particularly concerned was the frequently forgotten sheepdog – 'a highly-skilled worker who gets plenty of admiration but a low rate of pay and often . . . has to collect his own wages from a local rabbit-warren'.

The sheepdog had the toughest of all working lives.

They first raised the issue in 1944 and pursued it relentlessly, for they felt that the working dog deserved extra consideration even in those hard times. Under existing regulations, farmers had real difficulty keeping their dogs properly fed and thus fit for their arduous duties.

Some sheepdogs were denied their most basic rights in the way of food, shelter and freedom and in some areas endured – under the guise of ancient custom – such additional cruelties as having a foreleg tied up to prevent them from running the sheep too fast or a ring put through their nose so that they couldn't touch them.

The League pressed the new Labour Government to make more cereals available for working dogs like these; the problem had reached crisis proportions in the Highlands of Scotland and other hill-farming regions. In the autumn of 1946, the Department of Agriculture responded, allowing working dogs 28lb. of cereals a month – to be included in the official dogs' ration, National Pig Food No. 2, 'a mysterious compound with a cereal content which varies in amount' – but giving those belonging to hill-farmers and their shepherds an extra 14lb. (theirs was also a superior mixture, including flaked maize or maize meal). Marvellous news, said the League, but why penalise the lowland dog? They argued for an across-the-board 42lb. and for equal nutritional value in the two rations.

In 1947 the League introduced an extension to their veterinary aid scheme after gathering evidence that 'very many [shepherds'

The *Bulletin* regularly reminded readers about the special needs of dogs during winter.

dogs], particularly in the remoter districts, frequently suffer more or less permanently from worms, ear-canker, skin trouble and other complaints . . . Shepherds receive no subsidy of any kind and have little to spare for veterinary treatment.' Under the revised scheme, sheepdogs anywhere in Britain were to be provided with free medical care. The League also asked members to 'adopt' a sheepdog and pay for it to have a 'Sunday dinner' each week, a novel idea to which they responded enthusiastically.

Nowhere was the League's determination to keep going through the war and the tough years that followed better demonstrated than in the clinics. As has already been said, all those in the London area had been damaged by air-raids, but only one – that in Hackney – had been completely destroyed and even that eventually reopened in nearby Mare Street.

After the war, the League began slowly to expand its services. New clinics were opened in Eccles and Oldham, in Lancashire, and by 1949 the League had thirteen clinics at which a full hospital service was provided, including four in the north of England; there were also affiliated societies offering medical care in Cardiff, Ipswich, Plymouth, Worthing and York. In 1950 four mobile clinics were provided for the mining valleys of South Wales and the Bradford Animal Clinic handed over their operation to the League. Around this time, too, the Tasmanian Canine Defence League was formed in Hobart, affiliating itself to the NCDL and basing its structure on theirs.

The Sussex Home for Lost Dogs in Brighton, taken over by the League as a self-supporting enterprise in 1938, had been slowly rebuilt during the early years of the war. It stood at the corner of Robertson Road, in Preston Park ('a twopenny bus-ride from the sea-front') and in time became a dogs' hospital of great renown. Like the Hampton Home, it cost far more to run than it obtained in fees and had to be constantly 'topped up' from League funds, but it served a strong and devoted body of dog-lovers.

There were, of course, many human and canine heroes during the years covered by this chapter, as there had been throughout the League's history, but, unable to award their coveted silver and bronze medals because the metal was required in other, more vital fields, the League recorded none of them. In the act, therefore, must lie the satisfaction.

Nineteen forty-six, the first full year without war since Munich, was significant for the League for another reason – the retirement of C. Rowland Johns, Secretary since 1908 and editor of the *Bulletin* since its inception in 1920, after giving almost forty years of service

The Sussex Home, rebuilt as a model clinic and kennels.

to the cause of the League and the dogs it protected.

The loss of such a man from two key posts was a blow, especially as this was a period in which it seemed that the League was about to emerge from the darkness of the war years to reach new levels of achievement. The determination of the nation as a whole – symbolised by the Festival of Britain in 1951 – to set its feet firmly on a path of positive change and to rebuild the country's self-confidence by bringing both colour and ambition back into people's lives after a decade in which they had been able to do little more than survive, seemed to provide the ideal platform from which to launch a programme of renewal and expansion. For a few years this is exactly what happened. But then we come to the League's own private period of darkness.

Little or nothing can be told about the League's progress between 1951 and 1965 (only the 1953 annual report and an isolated *Dogs' Bulletin* survive), save to say that the organisation fell into the wrong hands, hands that were too aware of what they were doing to keep any record of their activities. In a few years they almost brought to nothing the entire work of the previous six decades.

Perhaps it is just as well that we cannot chart this passage in the League's history. This is, after all, supposed to be a celebration. What we can do – very much in the spirit of celebration – is to take up our account again in the mid-sixties (at which point the League, though they may have been in London, were certainly not swinging) to record a tale of recovery which ranks with the greatest of all their triumphs.

5 Out of the abyss

Recovery and expansion, 1964–1990

As they had always tried to do, the League put it plainly and simply:

> ... On 14 August 1964, by order of the Charity Commissioners, Mr Bernard Workman, Chairman, and Mr Jon Persson, Secretary, were suspended for a period of three months from the exercise of the offices which they held. They later tendered their resignations ...
>
> ... on 4 November 1964 [the Commission] appointed the following ladies and gentlemen to be the Council in place of the former officers: Miss Y. Anning, Miss Fay Compton, H. S. Stocks and W. G. West ... Mr Stocks [was] appointed Chairman and later Lt.-Col. A. H. RoosmaleCocq, MC, [became] Secretary. [The Council was later enlarged to include Sir Compton Mackenzie, OBE, Lt.-Col. Sir Thomas Moore, CBE, and Sir Jocelyn Lucas, Bt., KBE, MC.]

Lt.-Col. Alexander ('Rosy') RoosmaleCocq, MC, inspirational leader of the successful struggle to save the League.

Thus began the League's slow climb back from the abyss into which they had been plunged by an administration of whose activities mercifully little evidence has survived. It was to take two years of nimble-footed husbandry to get the League back to a level of financial stability from which development could realistically be contemplated, a period during which inevitably the needs of dogs, and particularly of strays, were not met with anything like the thoroughness with which they would normally have been able to tackle them. 'The League that saved the dogs' needed saving itself.

Although information about what went on during what might be called the League's 'Dark Age' is difficult to come by, one stark fact emerges from the accounts published in the 1965 annual report (the first for eight years): by June 1964 the League was in debt to the tune of almost £65,000.

It was a depressing picture. They had just two kennels in operation, at Watford and Brighton; one decrepit van which they couldn't afford to repair; and a staff reduced to the bare working minimum. The *Dogs' Bulletin* had been sold in April 1964. Membership was down to 2,500.

At least they still had a roof over their heads (now in Seymour Street), together with the will and enthusiasm of their army of helpers. Encouraged by this, the new administration – under the irrepressible Colonel 'Rosy' RoosmaleCocq, who was to be Secretary for another thirteen years, and Chairman after that – set about their task of cutting costs, raising funds and at the same time – and against many people's expectations – maintaining the surviving services: the kennels, the five remaining clinics in London, Brighton and Bolton, the centre in Cardiff, the postal training course, the Dog Spotters' Club for children, the advisory service and, when they bought it back in 1965, the *Bulletin*.

In the first year under Colonel RoosmaleCocq's management and the new Council's care, the deficit was reduced by almost half and by the summer of 1966, with the sports-loving population euphoric over England's victory in the World Cup and the famous Pickles proudly wearing the medal presented to him by the League for recovering the trophy in time for the England captain to hold it aloft, the League were celebrating their own more modest triumph. As the *Daily Mirror* reported:

> In just over two years [the League have] performed the neat little trick of turning a £64,000 deficit into a £6,700 credit. Conjuror-in-chief has been Lt.-Col. Alex RoosmaleCocq. 'I have spent the last two years pruning everything I could,' says RoosmaleCocq. 'At the same time, of course, we have kept up with all our commitments.'

Pickles, immortalised after finding the World Cup, receives his medal from the League.

It could not have been done without generous support from many quarters. Creditors withheld their claims and the *Daily Mail* chipped in with a free stand at the 1965 Schoolboys and Schoolgirls Exhibition at Olympia, where the League raised £250 in donations and subscriptions. It may be difficult now to appreciate just how much of a lifeline £250 could be, but such sums, painstakingly accumulated, enabled the League to clear their debts and start to think again about expansion. By the end of 1966 the annual report was confident enough to say that 'the salvage operation is completed'. The ship badly needed repairs, but at least it was seaworthy again. The time had come to make long-term plans.

The League were desperate to open more kennels, for the problem of strays and abandoned dogs, now their central concern, was becoming worse by the day. All kennels reported an increased workload (the Harrogate branch recorded thirty per cent more strays in 1966 than in the previous year) and the clinics were often overwhelmed, though of course they took in animals of all kinds: at

Croydon an average of 100 a week during 1966, sixty per cent of them dogs, many suffering badly from neglect at the hands of ignorant, even if often loving, owners.

Life was made particularly difficult by the deteriorating economic situation, but in 1966 the League reopened the Bridgend kennels in South Wales and in 1967 Heathercoombe Lodge, at Evesham, Worcestershire, became the first entirely new League kennels to open for many years. It was at this time, too, that Colonel Roos-maleCocq adopted a policy of non-destruction of healthy dogs, one the League has maintained ever since.

Tessa *(front)* and friend, helping out on Animal Flag Day in Brighton. *(Brighton Evening Argus)*

The Evesham opening was the outcome of a steadily improving financial situation, in its turn the result of hard work and good publicity. The League appeared at the Schoolboys and Schoolgirls Exhibition, the Ideal Home Exhibition and the Animal Fair, all in London, in 1967 and they had a share of the profits from the capital's Animal Flag Day, an annual fundraiser. The Brighton kennels had a flag day of their own in the town, and the money there was very welcome, for the Sussex Home provided a kennelling and medical service to an increasingly large catchment area. Pathé Pictorial, a popular documentary series which ran in British cinemas for many years, devoted issue no. 652 to the League's dog-training programme.

In 1969 *NCDL News* was launched with a circulation of 15,000. Its arrival was timely, for *Dogs' Life*, in which the League had had a page of news every month for four years, following the demise of the *Bulletin* in 1966, itself ceased publication in 1970.

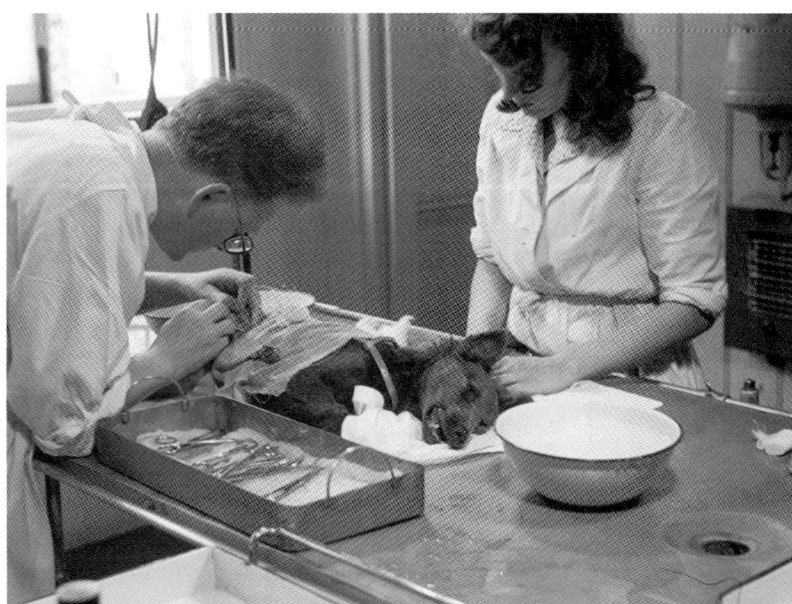
On the operating table at the Sussex Home clinic.

Lt.-Col. 'Rosy' RoosmaleCocq presents Inspector Willy Birch of British Rail with the League's medal for risking his life to rescue a dog running along an electrified line.

The disappearance of the *Bulletin* was a blow to morale, for it had been continuously published for forty-six years; but during the worst period of their financial crisis the League, after all, couldn't afford to keep it going. However, the *News* has proved a worthy successor, reaching its own twenty-first birthday in 1990.

Having recovered under 'Rosy's' guidance from the worst effects of those thirteen 'lost' years, the League's finances went from strength to strength. Annual income, just £30,000 in 1969, reached £100,000 in 1975, in which year net assets were £335,000, compared to a capital deficit of £10,000 ten years before, clear evidence of just how hard everyone had worked to pull the League round, for that decade spanned a period of national economic stagnation in which it wasn't easy for anyone to make good, let alone charities. (Around this time came the announcement of Colonel RoosmaleCocq's retirement, a severe blow, though he was not to stay in the wilderness for ever: in 1986 he was unanimously elected Chairman of the League.)

By 1980 annual income had reached over £300,000, a figure promptly doubled in 1981 (when legacies totalled £334,000). It continued on an upward curve until topping £1,000,000 in 1983 and has remained around that figure ever since. In 1988 legacies also exceeded £1,000,000 – thanks partly to the sale of Windrush Manor, in Oxfordshire, bequeathed to the League – and in 1989 rose to almost £1,500,000. Against a background of continuous inflation – rampant at over twenty per cent in the seventies – and enormous competitive pressure for money from other charities, as PR firms and agencies got their teeth into this new growth area, this was a staggering achievement.

Of course, that same inflation also affected expenditure. Outgoings quite often exceeded income as the League opened kennels not only in other parts of England but in Scotland, Ireland and Wales.

Membership of the League rose steadily from that low point in 1964: by 1989 the combined complement of members and donors had reached 80,000. As ever, subscriptions have been kept low: at the time of writing, they were a minimum £7.50 a year (£3.45 for senior citizens). The League have never wanted to be seen as an exclusive club serving only the wealthy but to remain an organisation open to everyone who owns a dog, no matter what their circumstances. Right up to their closure in 1980, service at the clinics remained free for those who couldn't afford it and the League continued to pay for dog licences for old-age pensioners and others in need until the licence was abolished in 1988.

The urgent need to find cash after the debâcle of the 'Dark Age' inspired the League's fundraisers, aware of the great tradition they were following. The annual Christmas-card appeal, launched in 1965 with the printing of 13,000 cards and some anxiety about

Carol Rainbird *(left)* and Fiona MacGregor, two art students, with their winning designs for League Christmas cards, 1967.

whether they would all be sold, was typical of the way the League's staff and helpers made a good idea work. Two Christmasses later sales were up to 50,000 and by 1969 had reached 200,000.

Other sources of revenue included the Lucky Dog Club, which in the grim days of 1965 realised a priceless £1,000. For 7s. 6d. every owner received an identity disc with their name and address, and the name of their dog, engraved on one side and on the other the League's guarantee that a dog injured while not in the care of its owner would receive medical treatment for which the League themselves would initially pay. Today membership is over 4,000 and owners who recruit new members are rewarded by the promotion of their dogs through the ranks: ten new members wins the dog the rank of 'officer', twenty 'captain' and forty a full generalship. The Lucky Dog Club is also a form of registration scheme.

The actress Fay Compton (a member of the League's Council) with Henry, who joined the Lucky Dog Club in 1967.

A story which perfectly demonstrated the value of the Lucky Dog disc was that of Rex, a nine-year-old with a dicky heart who got himself trapped in a badger sett while on holiday with his owners. After almost two weeks down the sett he finally dragged himself clear and landed, exhausted, on a stranger's doorstep. Only the fact that he was still wearing his disc enabled his rescuers to return him to his owners, who had been forced to give up the search.

As the League began to expand in the late sixties, concentrating on the opening of new kennels, fundraising schemes such as Support-a-Kennel, Give-a-Kennel and Donate-a-Bed were launched and the dog sponsorship idea was reborn, having had a brief previous incarnation as the Adopt-a-Dog scheme.

The *News* was originally set up in 1970 to 'sell' the Support-a-Kennel fund, which enables members to contribute towards the upkeep of a specific kennel unit. One of these 'homes' may be used by thirty dogs in a year and the maintenance costs are inevitably high; in 1970, the annual cost of maintaining one unit was £150. Today it is £500.

Donors to the Give-a-Kennel fund were offered the chance to have 'their' kennel named after them (or in any way of their choosing). Fifty pounds was enough to create a unit in 1970; by 1986 this had gone up to £300, but the scheme remains well supported, as does the Donate-a-Bed scheme, at around £50 per bed.

Further help was given to the League, as to all charities, by legislation: the 1972 Finance Act, for example, exempted gifts to charity from capital gains tax, including legacies up to £50,000, and new laws in 1981 relieved deeds of covenant of income tax and corporation tax liability, as well as increasing the capital-gains exemption on legacies to £200,000. The 1990 Budget also had good news for charitable donors in the form of the Gift Aid idea for one-off donations and tax relief for 'payroll' donors.

Each of the League's kennels was expected to raise at least some of the money required for maintenance, repairs and improvements and they tackled this annual task with gusto, organising open days, sponsored walks, fêtes and many other ways of persuading local dog-owners and sympathisers to help them in their work of rescuing and rehoming strays and unwanted dogs. The Kenilworth, Warwickshire, kennels set a remarkable standard in the late eighties when they raised £50,000 towards the cost of a major rebuilding programme, a sum matched pound for pound by the League. Even in areas where there were no kennels, groups of volunteers worked tirelessly to raise funds and publicise the work of the League.

Jilly Cooper *(extreme left)*, a staunch supporter of the League, with friends at a dog show at Downe House School.

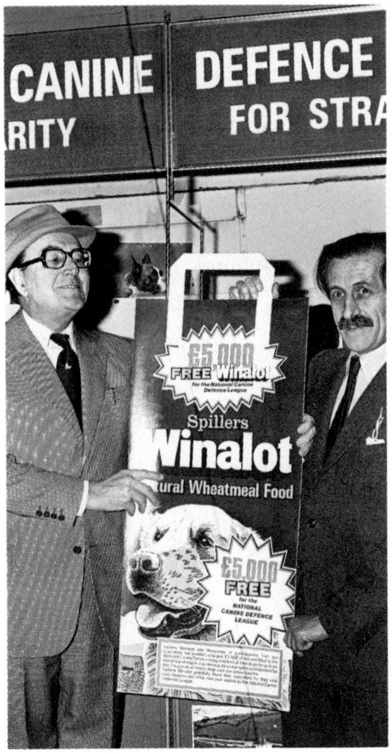

Council member Cyril Fletcher receives a £5,000 cheque on behalf of the League from Dr Alan Walker of Spillers. *(Marc Henrie)*

Recent ideas like the Dogathon in Regent's Park, launched in 1986, brought the League not only money but good publicity as, led by Council member, journalist and author, Jilly Cooper, and sent on their way by dog-loving celebrity Katie Boyle in front of the TV cameras, several hundred sponsored owners and their dogs set off round the park (all, we can be sure, with their pooper-scoopers handy). In 1983 there began the nationwide sponsored dog walks, the 'Walkadogs', which are now an annual part of League life. The League also participates in National Pet Week events every year.

Publicity became increasingly high-profile in the 1970s and many dog-owning stars of stage, radio and television were happy to lend their support, taking TV cameras along to the various kennels or encouraging members through the pages of the *News*.

In the modern way, the League obtained sponsorship from various manufacturers: a Pedigree Chum on-label appeal raised £20,000 in 1986, for instance, as did Quaker-Latz's sponsorship of the Evesham kennels. By 1987 the League had appointed a fulltime fundraising officer, and in that same year £180,000 was raised. The biggest single cash-raiser was usually the annual raffle, begun in the seventies and by 1988 putting £46,000 into the kitty.

The money was certainly needed. When the League put up the cost of subscription to £5 in 1980, inflation had risen 260 per cent since the previous increase. Small wonder that by the end of the eighties the *News* was devoted largely to reports and ideas on fund-raising.

And there were, inevitably, unforeseeable financial burdens to be born. Parvo virus, for instance, doubled the League's veterinary bills overnight, all dogs in their kennels having to be inoculated.

The health both of dogs and of humans coming into contact with them has been a persistently worrying theme of the last twenty-five years. Rabies, fortunately, has not been a major problem in Britain for a long time, although news of cases in Europe from time to time excites anxiety on this side of the Channel; but in 1970 the death from the disease of a dog in Camberley, Surrey, threatened to create widespread panic as owners in the area rushed to have their pets destroyed. Swift action by the League, who set up an advice centre in the town, averted the mass extermination of many perfectly healthy animals; they also paid for the quarantining of a number of dogs whose owners could not afford the kennelling fees, particularly as the Government insisted on the normal six-week period being extended to eight.

Greater worries than rabies were parvo virus and toxocara canis, though clinical research offered some hope that answers to both would be found. In 1980 a vaccine against parvo virus was put on the market. It had to be given to puppies at around six weeks and needed an annual boost. Although dogs did sometimes succumb to the

Minnie and her six puppies, found by a roadside in 1988. Minnie had a broken femur and pelvis and four of the puppies died of bronchial pneumonia caused by exposure. Their owner was never traced. All the League's kennels could tell similar stories of callously abandoned dogs. *(David Hartley)*

disease despite having been vaccinated, such incidents were rare (one case in 20,000); a bigger problem was that half the dog population simply weren't vaccinated against it at all.

Toxocara canis, the common roundworm in dogs, are passed in the faeces. They need to lie for two–three weeks in the soil before becoming infective. When infective they contain larvae which are released into the intestine if the egg is swallowed by a puppy. The larvae then migrate through the intestinal wall to various parts of the body. Some lie dormant in the tissues, to be 'reawakened' in times of stress such as pregnancy in the bitch or illness; others continue to full development, returning to the intestine via the windpipe, thus completing the life-cycle. Puppies can also be infected in the mother's womb via the placenta, and also by the mother's milk.

Regular worming of puppies, and less frequently of adult dogs, is, as the League constantly remind members in their efforts to encourage responsible ownership, essential to prevent infection not only in dogs but in humans, for if infected eggs are swallowed by a child, the larvae released could follow a similar migratory process to that which occurs in the puppy (though never to full development), lodging again in various parts of the body, including on rare occasions the back of the eye: this can cause partial loss of vision and even loss of sight in the affected eye.

Regular worming, which is simple, safe and effective, accompanied by routine hygiene in the home, reduces the risk of human infection to an absolute minimum.

* * *

League mascot Major at the mobile clinic in London in the 1970s. Also present are 'Rosy' RoosmaleCocq and Norman Horn.

Concern for the health and welfare of dogs, especially those belonging to the poor owners, had been at the heart of the League's original idea in opening their clinics after the First World War. It was therefore one of the sadder days in their history when they had to close down the last of them ten years ago.

The Fulham clinic had come under threat of compulsory purchase by the local council in 1967. Although it survived for a while (the slow machinations of local government working to the advantage of dog-lovers for a change) and in 1970 took in its 100,000th patient, it finally had to close in May 1974 after forty-four years of continuous service to the local community.

The mobile clinic serving Hackney and Camberwell had replaced the 'static' clinic in Hackney in 1958; ten years later it thought nothing of dealing with 5,000 animal patients a year, its blue-and-white League van (not the rusty relic from 1964) a familiar sight in the streets of East London.

When the Fulham clinic closed, Leonard Tillbrook, who had been its veterinary 'guru' since 1939, moved to Croydon, the clinic there going full-time, and when Mr Tillbrook died in 1976 Norman Horn divided his time between Croydon and the mobile clinic, which in addition to its normal duties appeared at Cruft's and other shows. Two years later the mobile clinic, in its twentieth year, also attended its 100,000th patient. At that time the three clinics between them were taking in up to 12,000 patients a year.

The crunch came in 1980, when Norman Horn retired after over forty years with the League and Peggy Brand, who had provided veterinary care at the Brighton clinic since 1947, also called it a day.

The President presents Norman Horn with his richly deserved Phyllis Mayer Argus Medal on his retirement in 1980.

The League were determined, despite this double blow, to keep the clinics open. 'We are confident that we shall be able to achieve this through the generosity of our supporters and the cooperation of the BVA,' said Lt.-Col. Wylie in 1979. His confidence was not rewarded. The British Veterinary Association insisted on the clinics providing a twenty-four-hour service, but the League could not find the staff to manage this. Croydon, Brighton and the mobile clinic were therefore closed in 1980 and a vital part of the League's service to animal-lovers was brought to a disappointing end after half a century of extraordinary achievement.

These days most of the League kennels have hospital blocks, so that a medical service is maintained in one important form, but these facilities, vital as they are, are no substitute, particularly in London, for the loss of that daily contact with local communities which made the clinics so popular. They acted as both hospitals and advice centres to every animal and every owner in need in their localities and enjoyed in abundance what today would be known as 'street cred'.

The dog licence cost 7s. 6d. in 1878 and exactly the same ninety years later – not, however, for want of opinions in favour of an increase. In 1966 a newspaper campaign stressed the old argument that a 'realistic' rise in the tax would not only make a more sensible contribution to the cost of collecting it but would automatically bring about a reduction in new dog ownership and thus bring down the number of strays.

Visitor no. 100,001 to the Fulham clinic is welcomed by vet Leonard Tillbrook in 1970. The 100,000th presumably nipped in before the cameraman arrived, too shy for his moment of fame.

The League pointed out that it might also deter a large number of existing owners, many of whom would probably prefer to chuck out their dogs rather than pay a higher tax, thus adding to, rather than diminishing, the stray population.

Fine, said the pro-risers, then try this: an increase could be used to provide a much-needed dog-warden scheme, under which trained men and women would be employed by local councils to round up strays and generally keep the 'dog problem' under control.

The League's answer was that a tax which truly paid for such a scheme would have to go up to such a level that only the very rich would be able to afford to own a dog. They still preferred to see the problem of unlicensed and homeless dogs tackled by the introduction of licensing at two months, not six, coupled with much stricter enforcement of the law on the wearing of collars and identity discs, as well as a greatly increased emphasis on canine birth control, particularly through the spaying of stray cross-bred bitches.

In 1969 they joined with the RSPCA, the Kennel Club and the National Farmers' Union in trying to thrash out a coherent plan to put before Parliament before the wrong sort of legislation was introduced, and the following year it was put to the Ministry of

Agriculture that the licence should be introduced at either the first change of ownership or six months, whichever came first, and be issued in the form of a metal tag whose colour or design would change annually, making it easy to identify tax-dodgers (very much the idea C. Rowland Johns had seen in operation in New York thirty years before).

The Minister was unmoved, so once again all concerned got their heads together and in 1971 the League, unable under Charity Commission rules to spend money on promoting legislation, were happy to see the Kennel Club sponsoring an amendment to the 1959 Dog Licence Act which involved a very simple idea: the dog licence would remain at its present annual figure but would run for three years.

This would increase the initial outlay and thus, everyone hoped, deter frivolous buyers, but would add nothing to the overall price. (Dogs for the blind and sheepdogs would continue to be exempt.) It would also cut down dramatically on administration costs. In addition, the new Bill would make it an offence to buy a dog without getting a licence and to sell one without ensuring that the purchaser had a licence, too. What pleased the League was that none of these provisions penalised existing, law-abiding dog-owners.

This Bill went the way of all too many before it, but good news came in 1974 with the setting-up of the Canine Consultative Council and the Joint Advisory Committee on Pets in Society (JACOPIS) – the idea of the British Small Animal Veterinary Association – both of which bodies were brought into being with the intention of improving existing laws and both of which counted 'Rosy' RoosmaleCocq among their founder-members.

In 1975 JACOPIS produced a major report, 'Dogs in the United

The League at Cruft's, 1973.

The actress Julia Lockwood presents a posthumous award to Kyler on behalf of his guard-dog predecessor Leo, killed while in pursuit of an intruder, *c.* 1970.

Kingdom', for the benefit of the Department of the Environment's Inter-Departmental Working Party on Dogs. Among other things, it recommended a licence fee of £3 per annum for a minimum of five years, with the usual exemptions and help given to needy owners through the social services; a change in the law to make it necessary to buy a licence at three months or on first change of ownership, whichever should come first; and an insistence that prospective owners should already possess a licence, very much along the lines of the Kennel Club's intended change to the 1959 Act. JACOPIS also proposed that local authorities should take over at least some of the responsibilities for collecting the tax, using the revenue to finance existing obligations to animals within their boundaries.

The Minister for the Environment, Denis Howell, seemed reluctant to introduce legislation on wardens, preferring to leave it to local-authority discretion. However, it did look likely that the Government would raise the licence fee. If this was done without using the extra income to finance a national warden scheme, felt the League and their friends (who were now basically in favour of such an idea, the emphasis in the warden's job having shifted from that of dog-catcher pure and simple to a much more educational role), it 'would undoubtedly be a tragedy', as the annual report for 1978 put it.

By 1984 the licence was bringing in £1 million in revenue but costing £4 million to collect and at last the Government decided to act, proposing that local authorities should be responsible for collecting a much higher tax, proceeds from which would go not to the Exchequer but to schemes to help dogs and the public. 'A £5 fee, we feel,' wrote C. G. Wylie, the Secretary of the day, in support of this idea, 'is a realistic sum which any dog owner should be prepared to pay.' (It was already £4 in Northern Ireland.)

However, there was now a strong feeling abroad that the licence fee should be abolished altogether, the argument running that only half the dogs in the country were licensed anyway and, if the cost went up, even fewer owners would bother to pay the tax, confident in the knowledge that they were highly unlikely to be prosecuted. The League argued that the higher fee could go to finance a national dog-warden scheme and wardens would be responsible, among other things, for checking on licences; the coloured-tag identity-disc idea, still very much alive, would make it easy for them to spot transgressors.

It was also claimed that law-abiding dog-owners would object to paying a higher fee to cover the faults of less responsible people, but Lt.-Col. Wylie would have none of this. 'We feel', he told members, 'that the vast majority of dog-owners . . . want to see *all* dogs properly cared for, trained to be well behaved and not be a nuisance to the public.'

Dame Janet Fookes MP, Parliamentary champion of animal rights.

'Privileges and responsibilities go hand in hand,' added Lt.-Col. Wylie in a reminder that seems more pertinent today than ever. 'Dog owners should accept that the benefit of their dogs' affection, loyalty and companionship carries with it the obligation firstly to safeguard the dogs' welfare and secondly to [see that they] cause no trouble to others.'

In 1987 the Government announced that it was indeed going to abolish the licence fee. The League repeated its misgivings, adding that abolition would 'open the floodgates to more misery and suffering' and give unscrupulous breeders and dealers an almost free reign to churn out puppies as from a sausage factory. They insisted that a licence fee of £5 was still the best idea and would help to finance not only dog wardens but a national dog-registration scheme.

At the time of writing (July 1990), such a scheme at last looks on the cards. The House of Lords has passed the necessary Bill – originally introduced in the Commons by longstanding League supporter, Dame Janet Fookes MP – and, although it could yet be vetoed by the Government, the League are optimistic that this vexed question is about to be resolved in a way which will do much to reduce Britain's toll of abandoned and destroyed dogs.

'The League gets asked what it is going to do about puppy farming, bad boarding kennels, backstreet dealers, licence evaders, puppies as prizes, sheep worrying, the number of road accidents involving dogs, unattended guard-dogs, and a variety of similar questions,' said an annual report a few years ago. 'The answer is as depressing to receive as it is to give. We can do nothing of lasting worth without the backing of tighter legislation.'

Although the League were unable as a charity to actively promote new legislation, they could, and did, make recommendations to the relevant parties, or, as in the case of the Licence Act, support someone else in their efforts to bring about what they felt were essential changes.

The Animal Boarding Establishment Act 1963 was an early object of their concern. In 1967, working alongside other groups, they sought to have closed the loophole through which kennels which were not purely boarding kennels were able to avoid complying with the Act's requirements on standards of accommodation by claiming that they offered only overnight facilities. MP Geoffrey Johnson-Smith supported the Bill in Parliament but it proved impossible to get it even a first reading.

The League did manage to get an amendment made to the Deer Bill in 1977 under which it had been proposed to destroy dogs whose owners had been convicted of deer poaching: not the first time it had been thought reasonable to make the dog pay the price

A typical puppy-farm scene: dogs housed in cramped, dark and dirty conditions. *(Puppy Watch)*

for the master's transgression. This was eventually rescinded to forfeiture and the League offered to take in all such animals, re-train them and find them new homes.

The guard-dogs issue was tackled in the early 1970s. 'We would like to see legislation introduced to forbid the use of unattended guard-dogs,' said the *News* in 1974. In the same year the League were closely involved in the drafting of the first-ever Code of Practice for the Use of Guard Dogs.

The Breeding of Dogs Act 1974 was aimed at discouraging puppy farming but affected honest small breeders much more seriously. The League campaigned with other groups to have it amended to make it effective against its intended targets, unlicensed and badly run 'dog factories', but the problem seems to be getting worse. No one who heard the *You and Yours* Radio 4 broadcast in October 1989 or followed the RSPCA's campaign in the same year can fail to have been moved by the plight of so many dogs and bitches kept in appalling conditions simply to breed puppies for sale on to an already flooded market.

Lord de Clifford, a member of the League's Council, raised the issue of dogs in parks in the Lords in 1977, following a ban on them in Burnley, Lancashire. There was growing anxiety about the risks to humans, particularly children, of catching toxocara canis, worms or salmonella from contact with dogs in public spaces, especially through their faeces. (The National Trust's recent banning of dogs on some of their beaches is another manifestation of continuing public anxiety, though the League feel this is exaggerated and have made representations to the Trust over the ban.)

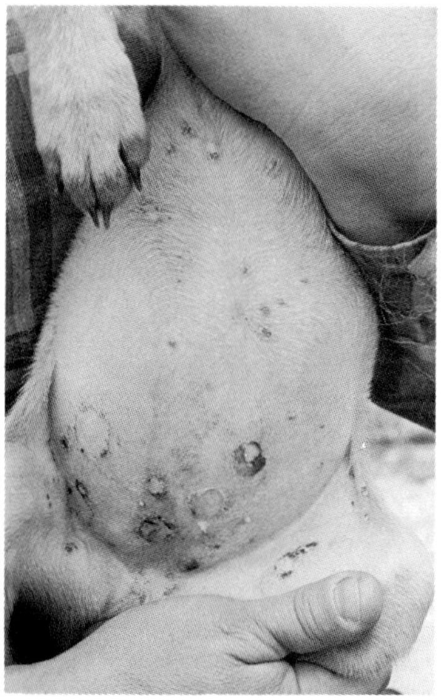

The kennel staff get a lot of fun from their dogs, but they also have to deal with this kind of thing: a dog repeatedly tortured with cigarette burns to her stomach. After two months with the League, she was back to full health and happily rehomed.

In his 1977 speech, Lord de Clifford called the suggestion of a ban in parks (except in children's playgrounds) 'a gross interference' with the freedom of a third of the population to exercise their dogs, though he agreed that something certainly had to be done about the risks: regular worming was one essential step that dog-owners ought to take without being asked.

The League suggested a simple home-made 'pooper-scooper' which could be conveniently carried when exercising dogs in public places. As ever, while they would defend the rights of dogs virtually to the death, they would never defend any owner who showed a blatant disregard for other people's comfort and welfare.

The welfare of their own subscribers had been uppermost in their minds when they had introduced their own third-party insurance scheme many years before. In the sixties it provided indemnity up to £10,000. The Animals Act 1971 made such cover essential, for under it owners whose dogs caused accidents on the roads while not in their care could now be liable to claims for damage or injury. As a direct result of this Act, the League increased its cover to £100,000 in 1972, £250,000 in 1981 and £1,000,000 two years later.

The League were as ready as ever to draw attention to any act of cruelty they came across. Nor did it matter how far away the victims were. In 1969 they campaigned against the export of dogs to Japan, where there were no anti-cruelty laws. One of the more unpleasant customs in Japan was that of quite literally 'posting' an unwanted dog through a 'letter-box', where it slid down a chute into a basket, to be either destroyed or sold for vivisection.

The League compiled a report for the Parliamentary Animal Welfare Group, including evidence from Japanese animal welfare groups, but the Government felt unable to take any action over events taking place in another country. Gradually, however, more enlightened views have come to prevail in Japan itself.

In South Korea, where dogmeat is a delicacy, dogs were killed by slow strangulation, as this was thought to ensure tender meat. Guard-dogs exported to Nigeria were often so badly treated on arrival that they lived for only a few months. In China, dogs were banned from Peking altogether in 1982 and a mass-extermination programme put into effect. In the Philippines, live dogs were sold for food.

The League could take no direct action against such practices, but they lent their support to campaigns organised by the World Society for the Protection of Animals (WSPA), of which they were members and through whom local welfare groups could hope to exercise some influence on their legislators. (Personal action by President Marcos put a stop to the human consumption of dogs in the Philippines after representations by the WSPA.)

Miniature bull terrier Titch meets sheepdog Kim (whose owner, a Berkshire farmer, is in traditional garb) at a public meeting to protest at the export of dogs to Japan, 1969. *(Sun)*

Not that there weren't – as ever – plenty of examples of cruelty in this country to occupy the League. Had their kennel staff been inclined to terminal depression, they would have had every excuse to give up the fight. Almost daily they collected, or found abandoned on their doorsteps, dogs who had been the victims of the most appalling treatment. Examples can be picked at random from kennel reports throughout the period.

Even where the aim was not to inflict cruelty on dogs but to protect humans from them, the remedies could be excessive, as the League were always quick to point out. In 1976, for example, rent collectors in Carmarthen proposed to carry twelve-volt 'cattle coaxers' on their rounds to ward off dogs who wanted to start an argument.

'Not surprisingly', reported the *Daily Sketch*, 'the first person to leap to the defence of the dogs was Lt.-Col. Alexander Roosmale-Cocq, Secretary of the Canine Defence League.' Rather more surprisingly, the *Sketch* went on, 'Rosy' volunteered to test the contraption on himself and 'went staggering across the floor as the machine's twin prongs sank into his flesh.' 'Rosy's' verdict? 'It will probably do more harm to [the] rent collector than to the dog . . . As soon as the dog gets the first jolt from the prod, it is quite likely [to] rip the rent collector to pieces.' This alarming prognosis did

Buddy, a Pit Bull Terrier used in dog-fighting: note the torn ears and missing part of the lower jaw. Rescued by the League, Buddy later became a permanent resident of the Ballymena kennels.

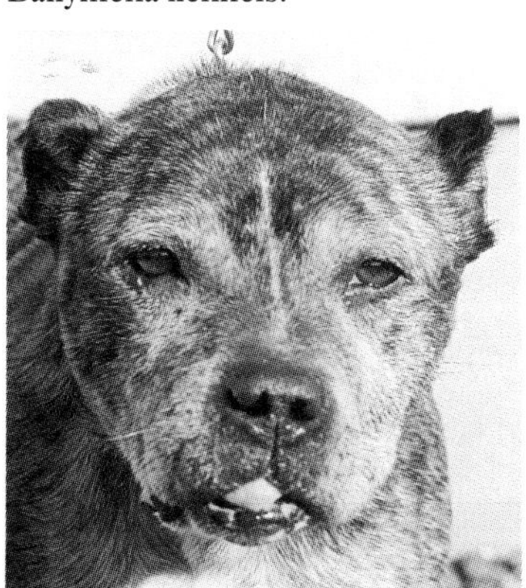

Every comfortably-off dog likes to have a country cottage in which to spend those quiet weekends away from the mad rush of the city. These two were waiting to be shown at Cruft's.

wonders for the rent collectors' sense of proportion and they found other ways of ensuring their safety.

As for vivisection, the *News* of spring 1983 made the League's position on that vexed issue clear: 'Sadly, the League neither has the money nor the manpower at present to delve into this matter more closely.' They did, though, ask members to report suspicious vans picking up strays ostensibly for the local council. The collecting of strays – often not strays at all – for sale to laboratories had a long and dishonourable tradition.

The League's main aim as they recovered from the devastation of the years before 1964 was to develop their network of kennels as quickly as possible and thus to rescue and rehome as many of the growing number of strays as they could. (In 1978 the Petersfield kennels alone took in 500 strays, most of whom were unclaimed – surprising, this, since up to a quarter of strays in all League kennels at any one time are pedigree dogs.)

This apparently admirable purpose was not as widely appreciated as you might think. 'Strays are delinquent dogs,' 'Rosy' Roosmale-Cocq was told in 1977. 'They should all be put down.' The NCDL, by refusing to destroy any dog in its care other than for health reasons, and by finding new homes for so many of them, were only making matters worse.

This view was typical of many; a lot of people saw strays as a ragbag army of scavengers roaming the city streets and the country-side, untamed and untameable.

The truth was, and is, that they are mostly domestic pets who have been abandoned and frequently maltreated and are only too happy to be rescued and found new homes, where they can become once more the faithful family friend, with no interest whatsoever in roaming, scavenging or any other delinquent pursuit. Dogs are eminently sensible creatures: they prefer a good hearth to a rubbish tip. The League have never had any doubt about the importance of their work.

Nor do they restrict their welcome to strays alone: they also accept dogs whose owners have either died or become too old or infirm to look after them any longer.

On arrival at a League kennel, all dogs are given a veterinary inspection and a full course of inoculations against parvo virus, hepatitis, leptospirosis and distemper. Most bitches are spayed before going on to new homes.

For the first seven days of their stay (if they haven't been claimed in the meantime), strays are kept apart from the main kennel blocks. Sick dogs are nursed back to health, badly behaved dogs rehabilitated.

Once the seven days are up, unclaimed dogs are offered to new owners, who are interviewed by kennel managers to ensure their

The League has always helped the poor owner if he cares for his dogs. In 1966 Donald Calver, a Hertfordshire recluse, was told his six dogs would have to be put down, as the conditions in which he was keeping them were not up to standard. Not so, discovered the League: Mr Calver's dogs were happy, cleanly housed and well fed, despite their primitive surroundings. With the League's help, Mr Calver won his appeal.

suitability. When time permits, a potential new home will be visited by kennel staff. All being well, the new owners sign an adoption form and the stray goes off to start a new life.

Should a dog not adjust to his new surroundings, the owners are required by the terms of the adoption to return him to the League. The form also makes it clear that dogs cannot be passed on to third parties without the League's consent.

Dogs unclaimed and for whom new homes cannot be found are never destroyed on any other than health grounds. They become permanent residents of the kennels. The Dog Sponsorship fund exists specifically to provide for these dogs. Sponsored dogs often spend the rest of their lives in the kennels, happy and much loved –

and frequently put in good work as foster-parents for new arrivals.

Spaying of bitches in the League's care, which currently costs an average of around £50 a dog, is paid for out of the Spaying Fund, which was started in 1971 with a donation of £250 by the Hamilton Fellows Trust. By 1988 the League were spending £26,000 a year on this vital work, whose importance can hardly be over-emphasised: in the late 1980s, it was claimed, as many as a thousand dogs were being destroyed *every day* in Britain. Anything that controls the birth of unwanted dogs is a positive step towards reducing the cases of misery with which the kennels are so often greeted when they open their doors in the mornings.

The League's kennels really need a book to themselves. All we can do here is to give a brief celebratory account of their development to date.

In 1964 the League had just two kennels in operation, the Ilmer kennels at Bushey, near Watford, and the Sussex Home in Brighton. The following year Bridgend was reopened and the League were also looking for premises in the Warwickshire and Worcester areas.

The Watford kennels were close to the M1 and were regularly called out to rescue dogs found wandering along the motorway, thrown out of cars by owners who had discovered that endearing puppyhood didn't last for ever or alternatively that the old dog had had his day, and really, what *do* you do with them? They also housed the League's few permanent canine residents and maintained a dog cemetery.

'Really, I wasn't *that* filthy!' A wash and brush-up for a new arrival at one of the League's kennels.

Unfortunately, they were badly sited and the police made no use of them, with the result that the League were forced to sell them off in 1969. The cemetery, however, was safeguarded and has recently been extended: it was featured in the *Daily Telegraph Magazine* early in 1990.

The self-supporting Sussex Home took in 300 strays in 1965 and the clinic treated over 5,000 animals, 3,500 of them dogs. This home, too, was badly positioned now that Brighton had expanded so much; what had once been a rural retreat was surrounded by houses on three sides and a railway on the fourth. Attempts to find new premises, however, were to be frustrated for years.

The Sussex Home actually reported slightly fewer strays in one year, 1971, but this trend didn't last and the kennels and clinic were at full stretch almost continually under the guiding hand of Peggy Brand, who had been manager of both Home and clinic for over thirty years when she finally retired in 1980.

In the mid-1980s the search for a new site focussed on Lancing, along the coast. A petition went round among local residents *against* the closure of the Preston Park site, and the League did in fact postpone the hunt for a year until, with the help of Brighton council, they at last found what they had been looking for at Goring-on-Sea, where new kennels (part of an existing establishment) were opened in April 1986.

The League's President opens the new Goring kennels in 1986. Was the dog a little reluctant to sit still, do you think?

The people of Brighton, including the police and environmental health officers, were glad to hear that the old premises were to be kept open at least for a while, to take in dogs whose owners found Goring too far to get to and to keep old, sick and nervous dogs for whom a move would have been traumatic.

But two kennels could not be kept open indefinitely, and in October 1988 the Sussex Home, founded in 1884, was finally abandoned and both it and Goring moved lock, stock and barrel to the newly purchased South Saxon kennels, in nearby Shoreham, an easy bus ride from the centre of Brighton. Opened by the League's President, Her Grace Lavinia Duchess of Norfolk (in her twentieth year of office), South Saxon had space for 100 dogs and boarding for both dogs and cats.

The Bridgend kennels, reopened in 1966 after extensive repairs, took in strays from thirty-four police stations in Glamorgan. Rehoming was a cooperative venture between the League and the

New arrivals at the Kenilworth kennels, 1990.

local RSPCA under a longstanding friend, Inspector S. H. Hancock.

The kennels had their whole future threatened in 1970 when the local council refused to renew their boarding licence after complaints about noise, but the League successfully appealed against an injunction. In that same year the Cardiff reception centre was forced to close following the death of the devoted Mrs Clutterbuck, who had run it for years in that tireless way which typified so many of the League's supporters in the field.

The extension of the M4 through Bridgend in the late seventies meant more casualties and more strays, with no room to expand on the existing site, and in 1982 Council member Jilly Cooper officially opened new kennels housing seventy dogs at nearby Tonyrefail, on old National Coal Board property; they were refurbished to League standards, with the intention of closing down Bridgend.

However, the introduction of a dog warden in Bridgend, with its inevitable impact on the number of strays, made it impossible to shut the kennels there and in 1984 the League took the decision to keep them going and give them a £100,000 facelift. The refurbished kennels reopened in September 1985 and 280 dogs were rehomed in their first three months – convincing evidence that the decision to keep Bridgend open had been the right one. The ill-fated Tonyrefail, too, came under great pressure and twenty new units were added in 1984, not enough to meet the demand but all that the space available would allow.

The first entirely new kennels to be opened by the League as part of their expansion policy in the sixties was at Heathercoombe Lodge, Broadway, near Evesham, in Worcestershire.

Broadway, as it was generally known, opened early in 1967 and was soon taking in fifty strays a week, many of them through Margery Palin's remarkable Avon Dog Rescue Service, which shared the expense of running the kennels. Broadway already existed as a breeding kennels, but the League were obliged to reconstruct and enlarge the site to cope with the ever-increasing intake of strays, many of whom stayed in residence rather longer than their counterparts at other kennels: homefinding was much slower in this largely rural region.

Typical of the dogs brought in to Broadway (all the kennels can offer examples of the same kind) were the terrier bitch found tied to a hedge in 1976, soaked in diesel oil and partly burned, and the greyhound rescued from a municipal rubbish tip and so covered with sores that her tail had to be amputated.

Less typical was Benny, a two-year-old English Mastiff (a rare breed), who weighed fourteen stone and ate eight pounds of meat a day. When the League went to collect him from his elderly owner, who was no longer able to look after him, it took them two-and-a-half hours to get him into their van, his own reluctance compounded by the fact that he couldn't be lifted. In the end they had to sit him on a garden seat and push him into the back of the van – which he then all but tipped over on the journey back to Broadway.

Another Broadway resident of unusual character was Tessa, a German Shepherd, who in 1978 got herself lost in a blizzard and made her way eighteen miles across snowbound fields and lanes before being rescued and brought to Broadway, where she was eventually reunited with her owner. Even more remarkable than the

Shane, a German Shepherd twice condemned to death for allegedly biting children, is taken into 'friendly custody' by Lt.-Col. Roosmale Cocq. The League fought, and won, a case on Shane's behalf and he was reunited with his loving family, seen on the right.

journey itself was the fact that Tessa was twenty years old. Her survival was a tribute to caring ownership.

Rechristened Evesham (at least by the annual reports!), these kennels were typical in needing frequent enlargement (twenty new kennel units in 1981, for instance), as well as constant improvements and repairs to runs, drainage, sewerage, roofing, heating and other facilities – and regular bulk deliveries of dogfood, something taken for granted until the lorry-drivers' strike of 1978, when all the League's kennels found themselves hard put to it to keep their animals fed.

In 1980 a second League pet cemetery was opened at Evesham and the following year the League's own mascot dog, a cross Borzoi/Foxhound, named Czar following a poll of League members, came to live there. Czar, a handsome dog who became widely known through his appearances in Crufts' Personality Parade and on the League stand at the Horse of the Year Show, and was once introduced to the Queen, originally came to the Bridgend kennels with massive wounds following a road accident and was nursed back to health by Bridgend's devoted staff.

Czar, the League's mascot for many years. From a painting by Miss Shirley Warne.

Although Evesham could take up to 100 dogs by 1982, it was sometimes overflowing with 'guests'; yet somehow room was always found for them. The League eventually decided to rebuild Evesham to take up to 120 dogs, with all-brick kennels and a new hospital unit (paid for by the Dulverton Trust). The hospital block opened in 1988; work on the main rebuilding programme will begin in 1991–2.

Three years after Evesham opened, the League extended their complement of kennels to five. The kennels at Watford had closed,

The reopening of the Ballymena kennels, 1983, with Gerry Kelly cutting the tape. Also present are Secretary Charles Wylie *(extreme right)*, next to Clarissa Baldwin, the League's current Chief Executive, and *(second from left)* Field Secretary Anthony Chiesman, with kennel manageress Joan Moore to his right. *(Belfast Telegraph)*

but two more were opened, at Ballymena, Co. Antrim, where there had long been an active branch of the League, and at Shrewsbury, Shropshire.

Ballymena opened just after the present troubles in Northern Ireland began and these brought a heavy influx of strays ('We never have an empty kennel,' said the superintendent in 1972) and at the same time made homefinding that much harder. From time to time, too, electricity and water supplies would be cut off and food deliveries delayed. Nevertheless, the kennels were a welcome addition to the animal welfare services of that part of the province.

By 1978 Ballymena had been enlarged to accommodate thirty-two dogs and there was better news of rehoming, which was thirty per cent up; a few years later the kennels were 'adopted' by a local junior school, whose pupils became regular visitors and helpers.

Ballymena's staff had coped for many years with wooden buildings which had become dilapidated and were in need of replacement, and in 1982 it was decided to rebuild the kennels, at a cost estimated at £40,000, a decision partly influenced by the new Dogs (Northern Ireland) Order of 1983. This handed over responsibility for dogs to district councils, who were likely to turn to the League for help in housing strays collected by the dog wardens which were to come with the new legislative package. The local branch worked heroically to raise a good part of the money and the new kennels were officially reopened in September 1983.

But even heroes get depressed. 'I think we reached the depths of despair,' reported the manageress in 1983, 'when a crossbred Doberman, whom we later named Bunny, was brought to the kennels. His sides and hind legs were practically devoid of skin, he was obviously distressed and in great pain. The vet diagnosed friction burns and we concluded that these must have been brought about by being dragged behind a moving car . . . Three months later, his wounds healed, a beautiful new coat covered the affected area and a new home was found for him at a neighbouring farm. On a visit to see how he was faring, a black-and-tan tornado emptied from the house and launched itself into my arms, pinning me to the ground and covering me with affection. It was one of the happiest days of my life.'

A tornado of a more traditional sort almost destroyed the new kennels a year after their reopening. Repairs had just been completed when in 1985 came the new £4 dog licence in Northern Ireland, leading to a huge increase in dogs brought in by their owners, initially for destruction but usually, if the League could persuade the owners to change their minds, to be found new homes. They even made time to take in two kittens found abandoned in the centre of the road outside the kennels: a resident Collie happily fostered them.

In 1988 Ballymena held its first-ever open day, raising £600; of greater significance, perhaps, was the way in which Catholic and Protestant dog-lovers worked happily side by side to make the day a success. The League's only kennels in Ireland continue to go from strength to strength.

Edward Whitley officially opened the thirteen-acre Shrewsbury site in November 1970 and became a regular donor towards the cost of establishing and maintaining what were then the League's largest kennels. In 1972 the police reported a twenty-two per cent increase in strays in the area, a trend that was to continue, and naturally the Shrewsbury kennels bore the brunt. Strays included Irish Setters, Dobermans, Boxers, Poodles, Old English Sheepdogs and other pedigree breeds.

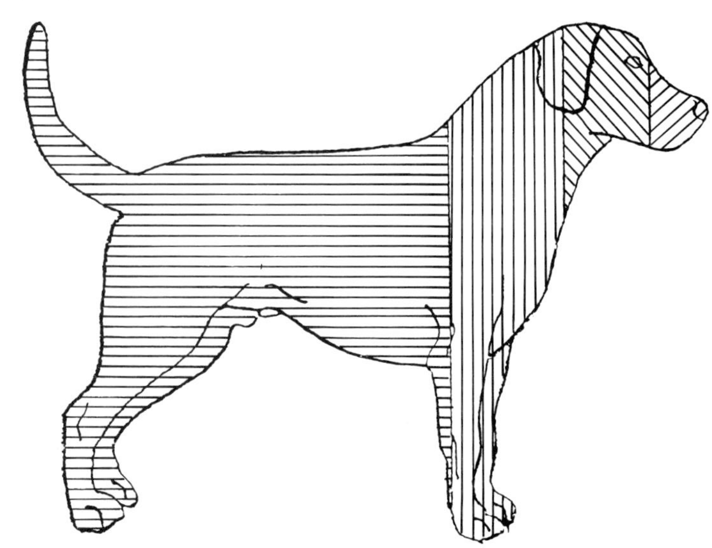

The League's work graphically summarised in 1989:

5,433 dogs rehomed (79%)

1,123 claimed (16.4%)

181 put to sleep or died (2.6%)

143 longterm or sponsored dogs (2%)

Search-dog Tarka at work with the Army in Northern Ireland. Working dogs, as well as household pets, can rely on the League to keep an eye out for their welfare.

In 1980 a programme of rebuilding began. The local environmental health officer would no longer permit wooden kennels and all had to be replaced by brick structures; these were paid for by W. G. Harvey, a local supporter, and through the Whitley Animal Protection Trust, who were to provide vital funds for Shrewsbury for many years; in 1987 they were characteristically generous in giving the kennels the £4,500 they needed to install a new heating system.

The arrival of 'an almost over-enthusiastic' dog warden in the area had its usual impact on the stray population and Shrewsbury – now called Roden – had serious accommodation problems by the mid-eighties, not for want of space but because of the prohibitive cost of continual expansion and the difficulty of getting planning permission to make the kennels bigger.

When Margery Palin died in 1973, she left behind an organisation, the Avon Dog Rescue Service, which had done extraordinary work on behalf of strays. The League were determined not to see this work abandoned and consequently took over administration of the service themselves, retaining the same team of volunteers.

The first priority was to find a new rescue centre for strays to support Evesham (or Wickhamford, as the 1973 annual report now called it: Broadway, Evesham, Heathercoombe Lodge, Wickhamford – you pays your money and you takes your choice, but they're all the same place!).

For two years the ADRS had been taking dogs not only to Evesham but to nine specially reserved units at Mrs Terry Ireland's kennels at Honiley, near the appropriately named Kenilworth, in Warwickshire. The League now built a further sixteen units there and, with Mrs Ireland in charge, the service blossomed, with the ADRS contributing towards the running costs as they did at Evesham.

The Roden kennels after refurbishment in the 1980s.

Broadcaster Kenneth Kendall opens the new Avon block at Kenilworth, 1989. Mrs Ann Woodall, Chairman of the League, is at the back, Jackie Cashmore, the manageress, on the left.

Terry Ireland receives her Argus Medal from the President following her retirement.

As ever, a remarkable number of residents were pedigrees ('Labradors, Great Danes, Cairns and Toy Poodles have rubbed shoulders happily with our crossbred inmates') and as usual many were dumped puppies, the eight-week-old found alone beside the M1 in 1975 being typical, as was the discovery of an abandoned bitch in whelp. So frequently did staff find puppies and older dogs abandoned at the end of their drive that it became habitual first thing in the morning to 'take in the milk and check the gate'. In keeping with League policy, Ireland's Kennels spayed almost all the bitches passing through their hands and neutered some dogs where necessary.

In 1978 the League put out an appeal on Radio Four's *The Week's Good Cause* for funds to expand their services. Among their most urgent needs was the money to purchase the Kenilworth property, for Mrs Ireland was about to retire.

In fact, she decided to postpone the sad day, but plans still went ahead to build eighty new kennel units – a wise move, for in 1981 new council rules in Warwick and Leamington Spa banning dogs from council properties led to the arrival of twenty-seven new dogs more or less overnight. But if the problem was acute, Mrs Ireland's cures were spectacular: she was rehoming 120 dogs a month by 1983.

Mrs Ireland finally retired in 1984 and the League bought the kennels from her, continuing to call them Ireland's Kennels as a mark of respect for her sixteen years of devoted service to dogs in the area. By 1987 they had become the largest of the League's kennels, with room for over 250 dogs, and in 1989 a programme of rebuilding had been completed with the addition of the Avon block for seventy dogs.

After Kenilworth came two more additions to the national network, at Newbury, in Berkshire, and Ilfracombe, North Devon.

Plumb's Farm, Hamstead Marshall, near Newbury, was officially opened in October 1974 and finally purchased outright by the League three years later. Its most famous resident was League mascot Czar, who later moved to Evesham, where he lived happily until 1987; he is buried in the Evesham cemetery.

Among the regular visitors to the new kennels was League stalwart, Council member and actress, Yootha Joyce, one of whose visits, to donate a new kennel in memory of her own dog, was commemorated on the cover of the *TV Times*. Her death in 1980 deprived the League of one of its most fervent and active supporters.

A new, £10,000 admission block was built in 1981 and in 1983 two dogs from Plumb's Farm joined the Hearing Dogs for the Deaf scheme; they included the scheme's first-ever demonstration dog, Favour. (Clarissa Baldwin, the League's current Secretary and

Actress Yootha Joyce, with other members of the cast of her television show, presents a League medal for canine bravery. Yootha Joyce was a member of the League's Council.

Chief Executive, is a member of the Hearing Dogs for the Deaf Council.)

Greyhounds – which, with Lurchers, seemed to predominate at these kennels – have always been difficult to place in new homes, but Plumb's Farm have been unusually successful in persuading potential owners of their merits, which are obvious to anyone who gets to know them. By 1989, following more rebuilding, forty-seven dogs could be accommodated on this spacious and thriving site.

'We're off to Devon!' said the *News* in the spring of 1972, but they weren't. Devon County Council refused planning permission for the site near Barnstaple which the League had earmarked for their first centre in the West Country.

It wasn't until May 1975 that Dame Janet Fookes MP, another Council member and later President of the RSPCA, was able to officially open League kennels at Hazeldene, West Down, near Ilfracombe. They had already taken in 258 dogs brought in by North Devon police since their unofficial opening two months earlier (only ninety-one were reclaimed).

The schoolboy who walked twenty miles to raise £30 in aid of Ilfracombe in 1975 got his blisters in a worthy cause: within a year 400 strays had passed through Ilfracombe's admission block and in the same year Dally, a cross Labrador/Dalmatian bitch, was the first NCDL stray to be trained as a guide dog for the blind. More sponsored walking, this time by children from Ilfracombe Comprehensive School, raised much-needed money towards the cost of building a new kennel block. In a year half the required £4,000 had been raised through such local enthusiasm; the rest was donated by the beneficent W. G. Harvey and his wife.

Favour, first League dog to be trained for Hearing Dogs for the Deaf, is seen here in 1981 with *(left)* American hearing-dogs trainer Pat Reilly and *(right)* Petersfield manageress Liz Wooltorton.

Ilfracombe even invented an alternative to the League's famous slogan from which the title of this history is taken. 'If You Don't Want the Dog, Don't Buy the Puppy' advised stickers generously distributed throughout the region in the autumn of 1979, just before the usual Christmas rush for a 'living toy' – not the only example of frivolous buying the kennels came across. Other problems included the annual dumping of holiday pets – the 'left-behinds', as the staff at Ilfracombe called them – and, at the opposite end of the spectrum, the holidaymakers who came to the kennels looking for a 'souvenir'. A live dog beats a china doll any day; if only they were always as well looked after.

By 1989 Ilfracombe had added twenty new kennels and a garden of remembrance and looked set to serve the needs of Devonian dog-lovers for a long time to come.

The Ilfracombe site before it was fully developed.

The League had wanted to offer shelter to strays in Scotland for years and in 1977 they finally opened kennels in Dumfries, simultaneously setting up an operation at the other end of Britain, in Petersfield, Hampshire. They now had eleven kennels, including the independent facilities used by the Harrogate branch.

Dumfries had room for forty dogs. Local support, under the leadership of Honorine Murray, who had been rescuing and rehoming strays in the area almost singlehandedly for years, was strong and Dumfries was soon thriving, proving a boon to Wigtownshire Animal Rescue and other welfare groups in the south of Scotland. A new hospital block was built in 1985 and an isolation block three years later.

Like all the kennels, Dumfries took in stolen dogs as well as

A grave at the Bushey cemetery. The League maintains three cemeteries, at Bushey, Ilfracombe and Evesham.

strays, usually delivered to the kennels by the police. These were the lucky ones – all too many were never recovered.

Petersfield became the League's largest kennels when it became operational at the end of 1977, with room for ninety-five dogs. It had been a thriving commercial kennels and the daughter of the previous owner became its first manager under the League. Major rebuilding began almost immediately, though not long after opening they were badly hit by parvo virus.

By the mid-1980s Petersfield had been almost entirely rebuilt, but suddenly the League, finding itself over-expanding in a tough economic climate, was forced to close down three kennels: Tonyrefail, Sheffield – and Petersfield, where the home-finding record was relatively poor in a predominantly rural area.

Some strays previously brought to Petersfield were now transferred to Newbury, and the rest were housed, at the League's expense, at local commercial boarding kennels.

In 1987 a block of eighteen kennels was opened at a boarding and quarantine kennels in Farringdon, near Alton, Hampshire. As usual, they were soon full, with a constant flow of new residents as dogs were rehomed in remarkable numbers.

The Sheffield kennels were probably the shortest-lived in League history. In 1983 Margaret Morrison was moved from the Brighton home to be the first manageress of Monny Brook Farm, Totley, on the moors close to the western edge of the city. Again, these were existing kennels, but again the League rebuilt extensively to meet their own high standards – each kennel needed twenty-four feet of shelter space and sixty square feet of run, and there had to be plenty of nearby grass for exercise. The Tailwaggers Club Trust contributed over £5,000 towards the cost of rebuilding and when completed the kennels had room for fifty-two dogs. There was no police contract, but demand was so great without it that it was probably just as well.

The Dumfries kennels, in lovely open country, 1981.

But then, in the winter of 1985, came a body-blow. New environmental health requirements were imposed, following complaints from nearby residents, and Sheffield was faced with a choice: move or close down. A long search for new premises came up with nothing suitable and after only three years in operation Monny Brook Farm reluctantly closed its doors in 1986.

Making use of existing kennels and helping to expand and improve them, rather than setting up entirely new establishments of their own, became League policy at the end of the 1970s, with the opening of a League rescue centre at North Farm Kennels, Snetterton, near Attleborough, Norfolk.

'It had become clear', said the 1980 annual report, 'that if we

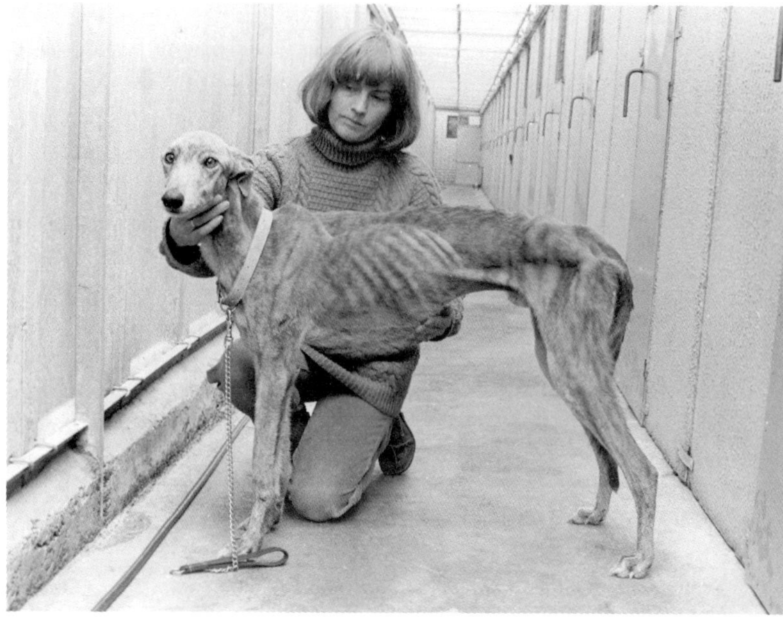

A starving greyhound, newly arrived at the Dumfries kennels, with manageress Jean Coupland. *(Dumfries and Galloway Standard)*

were to maintain and improve our existing kennels and staff conditions . . . in spite of soaring prices and a high rate of VAT, any new centre would have to be built where a kennel owner already in business was willing to take on a rescue operation in addition to his own work.'

Mr and Mrs Porter, of North Farm Kennels, came to just such an agreement with the League, who in August 1979 began operations in East Anglia for the first time. It was their smallest centre, with space for only twenty-two dogs, and not surprisingly was almost always full.

Several changes of ownership have had no adverse effect on the running of the kennels, whose only problem has been one of space – and publicity. They are well off a main road, but when they wanted to advertise their presence with a modest noticeboard at the top of the lane, the local council unaccountably refused.

Yet somebody certainly knew they were there. A new kennel block for fifteen dogs added in 1987 (along with a new isolation block) was full within days.

Yorkshire may have lost one kennels with the closure of Sheffield but they soon gained two more: Whitby and Leeds. Both were existing kennels whose owners willingly allowed the League to share them.

The North Yorkshire branch of the League was unique. The League's modern policy was to have no branches, but North Yorkshire, under Argus Medal-winner Truee Carr and her helpers in Harrogate, had been rehoming strays so successfully for years, and funding their entire operation without recourse to the League, that an exception was made in their case.

In 1981 Truee Carr retired and her work was taken over by the League, making use of the Adel boarding kennels in Leeds. Three years ago the League built thirty-two kennel units of their own on a vacant lot of the Adel kennels and at last the branch had substantially more space from which to run a remarkably successful operation (in 1988 alone they rehomed 843 dogs).

It was a resident of Leeds who, following the purchase of a number of small vans which were then decked out in the League's blue-and-white for use in kennels around the country, remarked that 'you seem to have vans all over the city'; in fact, they had just one in Leeds, but it was out and about all day, answering an endless stream of calls for help or delivering strays to new homes.

The arrangement at Whitby – another of what the League call their 'satellite' kennels – was similar: accommodation was set aside at Bill and Ann Edwards' Brackenhill Kennels for League use. The capital saved in not buying property could be used to rescue even more dogs, to which end the Whitby staff worked closely with the Whitby Dog Rescue Society, achieving what the League called 'a staggering rehoming record'.

Thirteen kennels in all four Home Countries: from their modern, purpose-built offices in Camden Town, into which they moved from Seymour Street in 1984, the League can survey their world and feel justifiably proud of their accomplishments over the past twenty-five years.

But if they have climbed out of the abyss and scaled a few heights, their Everest remains: to reduce the stray population and to put a stop to the ignorance, prejudice and apathy which has seen that population rising on a steady upward curve for too many years. The League's ultimate aim is as it has always been: to put themselves out of business by changing attitudes so drastically that services like theirs are no longer needed. Fat chance!

Truee Carr.

The kennels represent the cure, but prevention is what really counts and the League, while taking, as ever, a pragmatic approach to existing problems – expanding the kennel service; supporting training for dogs and their owners; striving for strong (and strongly enforced) legislation – still hope to influence the British public into accepting that dogs have a right to exist and to do so in comfort and in a caring environment.

'Dogs are a real and positive benefit to our society,' the League's President told members in 1982. 'Sheepdogs, guard-dogs, tracker dogs, sniffer dogs, guide dogs for the blind and now hearing dogs for the deaf . . . give enormous help to man in their different ways. Their value is easily appreciated, though it seems to be forgotten by

Kenilworth manageress Jackie Cashmore hand-feeds two new arrivals abandoned by their owners . . . *(Heart of England Newspapers)*

. . . while at the other end of the age scale, this twelve-year-old was rescued by the Plumb's Farm staff after his owner, too, found him superfluous to requirements.

the anti-dog lobby. The vast majority of dogs, however, ordinary household dogs, give even more to society . . . and it is this point which it is so vital to drive home.'

At the same time, responsibility must be exercised by all who enjoy, or profit from, dogs to see that their numbers don't get out of hand and that they cause the minimum of offence to other citizens, many of whom, it has to be acknowledged, are vociferous in their condemnation of most things canine, and in some areas with every reason.

The recent controversy over certain breeds of dogs has revived suggestions that all owners should have to accept training before being allowed to own any kind of dog, much as they have to take lessons before being given a full driver's licence. Compulsory courses in dog care, handling and training – which might well be encompassed in a single session – would not only improve the lives of many dogs, goes the argument, but, more importantly, would deter the more fickle among potential owners, bringing down the dog population (and the corresponding number of strays and chucked-out dogs) by reducing demand, which is all too often based on frivolous impulses and complete ignorance of what owning a dog actually entails.

The story of the National Canine Defence League's first century of work on behalf of dogs and their owners is not one of uninterrupted triumph. Many of the problems that existed in 1891 are still around. They may be insoluble. All the League can do is what they have been doing now for a hundred years, without stint and without once losing heart – face the problems head-on and find as many answers as they can within the limited resources at their disposal.

There are several organisations that help dogs and their work has been, and will remain, of inestimable value. But the National Canine Defence League is the only one that has for so long taken on the full range of responsibilities for the welfare of 'man's best friend'. If they have achieved anything, it is surely to have simply been there, trying to answer every need, in war and in peace, through every day of every one of those hundred years. No one could have done more. And no one will be striving harder over the next hundred years to improve the lives of dogs everywhere.

With eye upraised, his master's looks to scan,
The joy, the solace, and the aid of man;
The rich man's guardian, and the poor man's friend,
The only creature faithful to the end.

George Crabbe

6 No respite

The next 100 years

How do the League see themselves progressing as they approach the twenty-first century?

'On a day-to-day basis,' says current Secretary and Chief Executive, Clarissa Baldwin, 'the core of our work will remain rehoming and rehabilitating abandoned and unwanted dogs.' New rescue centres will be opened whenever the funds can be raised. Unhappy dogs will be given affection, sick dogs made better, bad behavers retrained; and all of them will be found new homes if it is humanly possible to do so.

But prevention, rather than cure, is the League's main aim in their perennial fight against neglect and ignorance. It has to be. Cures can only be effective in a small way. All the work of the League and other charities has done nothing to prevent a steady rise

The agility course: Yvonne and Steve Croxford put their dogs through their paces, 1990. The dogs are sponsored by the League.

The launch of the League's Roadshow, 1989. The Roadshow goes out to major centres of population, where the problems are greatest.

in the dog population to its present level of over seven million – that's a dog in every third British household. 'We will continue', say the League, 'to devote more of our resources to tackling the root of the problem – too many dogs for too few good homes.'

There will be an increased emphasis on neutering, with the already established NCDL Neutering Roadshow going round the country, educating owners, encouraging them to have their pets neutered and even offering help with the cost of the operation.

Dogs have been getting a bad press lately and the League are keenly aware of their obligation to represent the interests of dog-lovers in a responsible and reasonable way. They will pursue the struggle against illegal puppy farming and make their feelings felt on the issue of 'dangerous' dogs, often the prime example of irresponsible ownership. It should be borne in mind that the 'danger' all emanates from the owners, not the dogs; Pit Bull Terriers, Dobermans, Rotweilers and the rest can be trained to be docile and friendly as well as useful. Viciousness is trained into them; it can be trained out of them just as effectively.

The League will also persist, along with other charities, in their campaign to get the Government to introduce a mandatory dog registration scheme, preferably through a collar and disc enforcible by law.

'Our ultimate goal', say the League, 'is to see that every dog in the country has a kind, loving home; that there is no cruelty, no thoughtlessness, no ignorance of a dog's needs or an owner's responsibilities.'

When all that is achieved, the National Canine Defence League will quietly close their doors for the last time, confident that their job has been done and that the selfless work of successive administrations and supporters over the past 100 years has been brought to a triumphant conclusion.

I wouldn't wish to get rid of Pooch for anybody. I like my wife, too, but in a different way.

John F. Spencer, Salem, Mass., USA, asked to choose between his wife and his dog

Index

Notes: Entries in italic refer to illustrations. 'NCDL' is used as a convenient abbreviation for 'National Canine Defence League', as are 'WWI' and 'WWII' for the two world wars.

Adopt-a-Dog scheme 88
Agricultural Hall, Islington 3, *5*
American Society for the Prevention of Cruelty to Animals 46–7
Animal Boarding Establishment Act (1963) 96
animal welfare movement 3, *3*
Animals Act (1971) 98
Anning, Miss Y. 84
'Anti-Dog Campaign' 28–30
Anti-Vivisection Society 12
Argus Medal, Phyllis Mayer 65
Automobile Association 63–4, *64*
Automobile Club (later RAC) 16–17
Avon Dog Rescue Service 105, 109

badger-baiting 61
Baillie-Weaver, H. 12, 15
Baldwin, Clarissa *107*, 110–11
Banbury, Sir Frederick 10–11, 14, 15, 28, 34
Battersea Home for Lost and Starving Dogs 20, 21
Bell, Ernest 65
Blunden, Edmund 36, 39
Boer War 5, 6, 7, 17–18, 24–5
branches, League 7, 85
Boyle, Katie 90
Brand, Peggy 92, 102
Breeding of Dogs Act (1974) 97
British Board of Film Censors 59
British Broadcasting Corporation 59–60
British Medical Association 50
British Veterinary Association 93
Broome, Reverend Arthur 3
Bryan, Benjamin 1–2
Buisson bath *1*

Cahen, Louis 54
Campbell, Mrs Patrick 77
Canine Consultative Council 94
Capper, Mrs W. Bently 65
Carr, Truee 114–15, *115*
Cattle Disease Order 56
'cattle-coaxers' 99–100
cemeteries 102, 106, *113*
centres, League *5*, 7–8, 48–9, 51, 114
chaining *8*, 9, 34, 39–40, 56–7, *56*, 75, *76*
Chiesman, Anthony *107*
Cinematograph Films (Animals) Act (1937) 59
Clifton, Miss M. F. 65
clinics, League 51–3, *51–3*, 54, 82, 85–6, *86*, 87, *93*; and National Canine Defence Week 55; in WWII 67, 71, *74*, *75*; mobile clinic 92–3, *92*; closure 92–3; *see also* Hampton Home: Sussex Home
collars 13–14, 19, 49, 58, 93; *see also* dog licence
Collie, Frank 54
Compton, Fay 84, *88*
Control of Dogs Order (1930) 46, 49
Cooper, Jilly *89*, 90, 104
cruelty, examples of 8, 55–62, *58*, *98*, 105, 107–8, 112, 114; legislation against 56, 57–8, 59, 96–7; in wartime 74; *see also* chaining; vivisection
Cruelty to Animals Act (1876) 3, 9, 12
Cruelty to Animals (Amendment) Bill (Forfeit Bill) 9–10, 11
Cruft's Dog Show 3, *12*, 60, *61*, *80*, *94*, *100*
Czar (League mascot) 106, *106*

de Clifford, Lord 97, 98
Deer Bill 96–7
dealers, dog 17, 21, 96
diseases in dogs 90–1, 97, 101
dog-fighting 61, 78
dog licence 5, 9, 44–7, *47*, 73–4, 87, 93–6; during WWI 30–2; in USA 46–7, 94; limiting period of 93; and sheepdogs 94; abolition of 95, 96
Dog Licence Act (1959) 94
Dog Licence Clubs 5, 19–20
Dog Licence Fund 18–20, 31–2, 43, 44–5, 73, 79
'dog-scares' 1–3
dog shows *5*, *12*, 60–1, 78
Dog Spotters' Club 85
dog wardens 93, 95, 104, 107, 109
'dog-wool' 71, *71*
dogs
in countryside 8, 56–8, 75, 81, 96; destruction of (by League) 6, 7, 22, 49, 52, 68, (illegal or illicit) 57–8, 96–7; and drinking water *17*, *44*; health of 42–3, 61, 90–1, 97, 101 (*see also* clinics; veterinary ticket scheme); licensing of *see* dog licence; and local councils 65, 75–6; ownership of 21, 101, 116; population of 46, 51, 117–18; and public transport 65, 78 (buses and trams 5,8,78; trains 17, *17*, 35–6, 64–5, 78); selling 17, 21, 33–4, 96; sponsored 101–2
Dogs' Act (1906) 13–14, 15, 19, 20
Dogs (Amendment) Act (1928) 49
Dogs and Cats Bill 49
Dogs (N.I.) Order (1983) 107
Dogs' Bulletin 36, *42*, 80, 85, 86–7
Dogs (Exemption) Bill 11
Dogs' Life 86
Dogs (Protection) Bill 10–11, 14, 34–5, 49–50; *see also* vivisection
Dogs Regulation Bill (1898) 1–2, 4, 6
Donate-a-Bed 88, 89
draught dogs *9*, *32*, 33, 61
Dulverton Trust 106

Ede, James Chuter- (1882–1965) 78
electric kennels 52

farm-dogs 36, 39
film industry and dogs 59, 78
films, League *see under* NCDL
Finance Act (1972) 89
finance, League *see under* NCDL
Fisher, H. A. L. 29
Fletcher, Cyril *90*
Fookes, Dame Janet *96*, 111
Forfeit Bill 9–10, 11
fundraising, League *see under* NCDL

Galsworthy, John 15, *15*
Give-a-Kennel 88, 89
Gower, Sir Robert 29, 49, 56, 59, 80
Grateful Dogs' Fund 54
Greenwood, Sir George 11
greyhounds 61, 76, 111
Griffiths, Ellis 13
guard-dogs 96, 97, 98, 115–16; in WWI 33; in WWII 68, 70
guide dogs for the blind 65, *65*, 69–70, 115–16; and dog licence 74, 94

Hamilton Fellows Trust 102
Hampton Home *49*, 49, 51, 54, 82; in WWII 72
Hancock, S. H. 104
Harvey, W. G. 109, 111
Hays, Will H. 59
health of dogs *see under* dogs
hearing dogs for the deaf 110–11, 115–16
heroes (canine) *21*, *23*, 24–5, *36*, 64, 82, *87*; (human) *18*, 23–4, *24–7*, 36, 64, 82, *87*
homes, League 54, 55, 79; *see also* Hampton Home; Sussex Home
Horn, Norman 92, *92*
Howell, Denis *95*
Hurndell, J. Sutcliffe 12

Ilfracombe Comprehensive School 111
insurance *see under* NCDL
Ireland, Mrs Terry 109–10, *110*

JACOPIS 94–5
James, Samuel 41
Johns, C. Rowland 6, 28, 34, 48, *59*; and Forfeit Bill 11; and 'Save the Dog' campaign 38–9; and dog licence 46, 94; and books 54, 65; retirement 82–3
Johns, Rowland (son of C. R. J.) 71
Johnson-Smith, Geoffrey 96

'Jolly Old Dogs Club' 54
Joyce, Yootha 110, *111*

Kekewich, Sir George 25
Kennel Club 58, 60–1, 93, 94, 96
kennels, League 84, 85, 87, 101–2, 115; medical facilities at 93; development 100; listed *viii*, 102–16
Knight, George 6, 11

Lambourne, Lord 28, 29, 49; as Col. A. R. M. Lockwood 15
Law, A. Bonar (1858–1923) 28–9, *28*
legislation 2–3, 4, 8, 9–11, *10*, 19, 62, 73, 89; and chaining 9, 40; and cruelty 56, 57–8, 59, 96–7; and dog licence 93–6; and quarantine 17–18, 35, 61, 78; and rabies 1–3, 4, 17–18, 34–5; and strays 49–50, 89, 107, 108; and vivisection 10–15, 34, 74–5; during WWII 69, 73
lethal chambers 6, 7, 22, *22*, 52
Licence Fund *see* Dog Licence Fund
Long, W. H. 1, 3, 4, 6, 17
Lucas, Sir Jocelyn 84
Lucky Dog Club 88, *88*

Mackenzie, Sir Compton 84
markets, street 7–8, 21, *21*
Martin, Richard ('Humanity Dick') 3, *3*
Million Sixpence Fund 6, *6*
Moore, Joan *117*
Moore, Lt.-Col. Sir Thomas 84
Morrison, Margaret 113
Murray, Honorine 112
muzzling 1–3, *2*, 4, 17–18, 34–5

National Canine Defence League ambulance, first motor 49, *52*: campaigns, major 4, 24–5, 39, 50, 64, 98 (against vivisection 10–15); films, promotional 48, 55, 86; finance 4–7, 38, 54–5, 78–9, 86–7 (donations and legacies 5, 39, 54, 78, 79, 87, 89; insurance for members 79, 98; membership 4–5, 78, 79, 85, 87, 88; sponsorship 28, 90, *90*; subscriptions 54, 79, 87, 90); fundraising 5, *5*, 6–7, *6*, *7*, 38–9, 54–5, 85–9, 90, 108, 111; offices 4, 12, 44, 71, 85, 115; origins 3–4; and the press 3, 34, 48 (support frcm 4, 12, 25–6, 45, 85); veterinary ticket scheme *51*, 53–4, 81–2;
see also centres; clinics; homes; kennels; shelters
NCDL News 86–7, 88
National Canine Defence Week 55, *55*
National Farmers Union 57–8, 74, 93–4
National Trust 97
National Veterinary Medical Association 52
Neutering Roadshow, NCDL 118, *118*
Norfolk, Her Grace Lavinia Duchess of vi, 103, *103*, 110, 115–16

Our Dogs 55

Palin, Margery 105, 109
parvo virus 90–1, 101
Pasteur, Louis 4
Performing Animals Bill 41
performing dogs 23, 40–1, *40–1*, 58–61, *58*, 78
Persson, Jon 84
Pirkis, Fred 5, 6, 8, 18
Pirkis, Norah 22
police *48*
and 'dog-scares' 1, 4; and strays 4, 7, 20–1, 51, 78; and chaining 39; and veterinary ticket scheme 54
population, dog 46, 51, 117–18
press and League *see under* NCDL
Protection of Animals Act (1911) 11
Protection of Animals (Cruelty to Dogs) Act (1933) 56
public transport and dogs *see under* dogs
puppy farming 91, *97*, 118

quarantine 41–2, 61, 76–7; and Boer War 6, 7, 17–18; and rabies 35, 90; and WWII 76–7, 78

rabies 17–18, 35, 36, 90
railway companies and dogs 17, *17*, 35–6, 64–5, 78
Red Cross 33–4
registration, dog 88, 96, 118
Richardson, Lt.-Col. E. H. 48
road safety 16, 64, 75–6, *77*
Road Traffic Act (1930) 64
RoosmaleCocq, Lt.-Col. Alexander ('Rosy') 84–7, 94, *100*, *105*
rounding of ears 61
Royal Commission on Vivisection (1875) 3–4; (1906–12) 14–15
Royal Society 8
Royal Society for the Prevention of Accidents 76
Royal Society for the Prevention of Cruelty to Animals 3, 59, 104; and dog licence 9; and Dogs (Protection) Bill 11, 50; during WWII 69–70, 72; and road safety 76

Salisbury, 3rd Marquis of (1830–1903) 2, 17
Salvation Army 7, 39
Samuel, Sir Herbert (1870–1963) 51
'Save the Dog' campaign 38–9
schools and dogs 25, 48, 55, *55*, *77*
sheepdogs 57, 80–2, *81*, 94, 115–16; *see also* dogs in countryside
shelters, League 20, 21, 39, 48, 54, 55
Sladen, Lt.-Col. Sydney 29
spaying 93, 101, 102
Spaying Fund 102
sponsorship *see under* NCDL
Stock, Lady (Gertrude) 3, 4
Stocks, H. S. 84
stolen dogs 20, 21, 50, 112–13
strays 7, 9, 20–2, *20*, *46*, 47–51, *48*, *50*, 84, 85–6, 100–1, 102–18; and Million Sixpence Fund 6; destruction of 7; and dog licence 19, 93; and Dogs' Act (1906) 13; in WWI 32–3; and 'Save the Dog' campaign 38–9; shooting of 57; and the police 4, 7, 20–1, 51, 78; and spaying 93; Stray Dogs' Fund 38, 39; *see also* shelters, League
Support-a-Kennel 88–9
Sussex Home 51, 60, 82, *83*, 86, 102–3

Tailwaggers Club Trust 113
tail-cropping 61
Tasmanian Canine Defence League 82
Tillbrook, Leonard 92, *93*
Toxocara canis 90–1, 97

USA, dog licensing in 46–7, 94
University College, London 12

veterinary ticket scheme ('Help the Dogs') *51*, 53–4, 81–2
Vivian, Margaret 54
vivisection 8, 10–11, *11*, *13*, *49*, 49–50, *50*, 74–5, 100; Royal Commissions on 3–4, 14–15; statistics on 14, 34; *see also* Dogs (Protection) Bill

wartime, dogs in 35, 68, *73*; behaviour of 24–5, 72–3; feeding 27–9; protection and safety of 28–30, 66, 67–8 (during air-raids 34, 72–3, *73*, *74*, *79*; during gas attacks 66, *67*, 68, *70*); and quarantine 7, 17–18, 76–7, 78; treatment of 27–31, *79*; uses of 18, 25, *31*, *33*, *35*, 68, *70*, 70–1
West, W. G. 84
Whitby Dog Rescue Society 115
Whitley, Edward 108
Whitley Animal Protection Trust 109
Wigtownshire Animal Rescue 112
Women's Voluntary Service 71
World Society for the Protection of Animals 98
World Wars: First 26–43; Second 66–82
Woolton, Frederick James (1st Baron) (1883–1964) 69
Workman, Bernard 84
worming 91, 97, 98
Wylie, Lt.-Col. Charles 95–6, *95*, *107*

Young Farmers Clubs 36

Zeppelins 34, *34*